Thomas McCants Stewart

Liberia: the Americo-African Republic

Being some Impressions of the Climate, Resources, and People

Thomas McCants Stewart

Liberia: the Americo-African Republic
Being some Impressions of the Climate, Resources, and People

ISBN/EAN: 9783337125691

Printed in Europe, USA, Canada, Australia, Japan

Cover: Foto ©ninafisch / pixelio.de

More available books at **www.hansebooks.com**

LIBERIA:

THE AMERICO-AFRICAN REPUBLIC.

BEING

SOME IMPRESSIONS OF THE CLIMATE,
RESOURCES, AND PEOPLE,

RESULTING FROM

PERSONAL OBSERVATIONS AND EXPERIENCES

IN WEST AFRICA.

By T. McCANTS STEWART,

*Former Professor of Mathematics in the South Carolina State Agricultural College;
Late General Agent for Industrial Education in Liberia.*

WITH AN INTRODUCTION

By DR. G. W. SAMSON,

Former President of Columbian University, Washington, D.C.

NEW YORK:
EDWARD O. JENKINS' SONS,
20 NORTH WILLIAM STREET.
1886.

THIS VOLUME IS RESPECTFULLY DEDICATED

BY THE AUTHOR

TO

HENRY M. SCHIEFFELIN,

Former Consul-General of Liberia for the United States of America,

WHOSE

INCREASING INTEREST IN THE GROWTH AND PERPETUITY OF THE
AMERICO-AFRICAN REPUBLIC; WHOSE UNSELFISH SERVICES
AND WISE COUNSELS FREELY GIVEN THE GOVERNMENT
AND THE PEOPLE; AND WHOSE LARGE AND
GENEROUS DONATIONS TO PUBLIC AND
PRIVATE LIBERIAN ENTERPRISES,

PLACE HIM FIRST AMONG THE AMERICAN FRIENDS OF THAT RE-
PUBLIC, EVEN AS HE STANDS FOREMOST IN SCHIEFFELINVILLE
IN THE REPUBLIC OF LIBERIA.

INTRODUCTION.

The Belgian king, who has enlisted the great States of Europe to follow his "New Star in the East" on the Congo, found his parallel to guide him in Berkeley's "Star of Empire"; which arose two and a half centuries ago on the American shores. In the history of Liberia the parallel holds good. The men who colonized the new settlements, now constituting the United States of America, were mostly the descendants of slaves under successive Roman, Saxon, Danish, and Norman lords. They learned self-government as colonists only after five generations of protectorate under the mother country. Their early settlements on the coast and along river-bottoms proved unhealthful, sterile, and inhospitable. Jamestown was soon deserted; Chester and Plymouth were left to decay; commerce often was hampered; and public debt seemed irretrievable. Youth were sent to the mother country to be educated; and churches sought both ministers and their support from the mother country.

Liberia was settled only two generations ago by slaves just freed, without property or education. In one generation they were nominally independent; having their own Executive, Judiciary, and Legislature. No nation behind, fully in sympathy, fostered them in their need; the U. S. Government only making their territory an asylum for recaptured slaves; and not even granting their special needs, exploration and opening up inland resources, mail communication with their kindred at home, a gun-boat to protect their commerce; all which "neglect" another Burke in the U. S. Congress is needed faithfully to portray. If Millsburg is deserted, and Monrovia decaying; if no sanitary safeguards are inaugurated, no harbor opened, and no wharf erected; if roads are not opened, and mineral resources are not developed; if territory purchased by the U. S.

Government is seized by European Powers, and Liberian commerce is monopolized; if interior settlements are not therefore made possible; if education is struggling both against ignorance and imperfect guardianship—not only the Americo-African, but the Anglo-American—yes, all Europe is asking: "Who for this is responsible? the colonists? or the nation whose lands have been tilled, whose cotton has been raised, whose mills erected, whose marts have been made busy, and whose treasury has been supplied from their half-requited labor?"

Another generation of Americo-Africans has arisen; whose claim to be true Americans outranks in length of time any other nationalities except the primitive English and Dutch settlers. In twenty years they have witnessed an advance in culture unparalleled in the annals of nations and races. They see the "New Star in the East" rising. They wish to know the practical facts as to its history and promise; for it is their "fatherland." If never to enlist in its redemption, it is as dear to them as is their own to Anglo-Saxon or German-Americans. Just now, too, the world's eye is turned to that land, the early seat of an advanced civilization; and they who hail it as the home of ancestry, wish to be assured as to its hope for the future.

He who reads thoughtfully, impartially, the pages that follow, will find just what practical Americans of all predilections need and desire to know.

What is vital in the work now offered the public, is its call to Christian thought. Burke, in 1790, *foretold* that the French Republic would *fail* from lack of Christian reverence; Senator Sumner recalled this forcibly to Jules Favre in 1872; and if Liberia is saved from disaster, it will only be by having public men like those who, in many a time of peril, have saved the American Republic.

G. W. SAMSON.

121 W. 125TH ST., NEW YORK CITY.

PREFACE.

This book is an honest endeavor to do some good. In it nothing is set down in malice; and yet its truths may be offensive to some. In writing it, however, I have never at any time paused for a moment to consider whether or not I shall please or displease anybody. My aim has been simply to set forth plainly and truthfully the situation as I found it in Liberia, so as to give information which may be of interest, and possibly of use, to others.

Many will criticise my work. Some will say I have minimized the difficulties attending life in West Africa, and exaggerated the resources of the country. Others will urge that I have been too much of an apologist; that I have not told the whole truth. There may be some force in this latter criticism.

True, I have not mentioned the dishonesty and incompetency of political officials. I have not told the story of a swindling loan contracted in England fifteen years ago, when the English money-sharks and dishonest Liberians preyed upon the Republic like vultures, stealing almost seventy-five cents out of every dollar borrowed. I have not recorded the fact that this swindle, which is not yet settled, may cause the British Government to assume a Protectorate over Liberia, as it has lately done over Egypt.

I confess that I have left much unsaid from the necessary limits of a work of this kind. But, although much has been omitted, I have said enough to awaken thought and inquiry which may lead to practical results.

If this should prove true, I shall take it to be an answer in part to the prayer I offered, when I stood for the first time in Palm Grove Cemetery, in Monrovia, at the grave of the illustrious Henry Highland Garnet, whose body lies near the shores of the Atlantic Ocean, which he so heroically crossed, in his old age, with a Message of sympathy and cheer to the struggling Liberian Republic.

THE AUTHOR.

81 Adelphi St., Brooklyn, N. Y.

CONTENTS.

		PAGE
CHAPTER	I.—THE AFRICAN CONTINENT,	9
"	II.—THE SEARCH FOR AFRICAN TERRITORY,	13
"	III.—THE STRUGGLE TO ESTABLISH THE COLONY,	19
"	IV.—CLIMATE—THE RAINY SEASON,	22
"	V.—CLIMATE—THE DRY SEASON,	26
"	VI.—CLIMATE—THE CAUSES OF UNHEALTHINESS,	30
"	VII.—CLIMATE—MALARIA DETHRONED,	35
"	VIII.—CLIMATE—AFRICAN FEVER,	40
"	IX.—RESOURCES—NATURAL AND CULTIVATED PRODUCTS—A GROWING COMMERCE,	45
"	X.—PEOPLE—THE NATIVES—THEIR CUSTOMS AND MANNERS,	54
"	XI.—PEOPLE—THE KROO AND THE VEY TRIBES,	65
"	XII.—PEOPLE—THE AMERICO-AFRICANS,	70
"	XIII.—PEOPLE—RELATION OF LIBERIANS AND NATIVES,	77
"	XIV.—PEOPLE—GENERAL CONDITION AND PROSPECTS,	83
"	XV.—MISSION AND EDUCATIONAL WORK NEEDED,	92
"	XVI.—AMERICAN INTEREST IN THE AFRICAN REPUBLIC,	100

CHAPTER I.

THE AFRICAN CONTINENT.

THE name "Dark Continent" has lost its significance. Africa now stands in the eye-flash of Deity and before the gaze of the civilized world. Exploration and commerce have opened the mouth of the Sphinx, and there is no longer deep-veiled mystery enshrouding the land of "Ethiopia's blameless race." Mungo Park, Livingstone, and Stanley have penetrated its swamps and its forests, traversed its lakes and its rivers, and have told us what they revealed unto them.

Even the name of this great continent has been a subject of much discussion. It is believed that it is derived from the Latin word *Aprica* (sunny), or the Greek word *Aphriké* (without cold).

Africa lies between the latitudes of 38° N. and 35° S. More of its surface is within the tropics than that of any other of the continents. It is larger than Europe or Australia. In its physical conformation it may be compared to an upturned plate or saucer. It slopes at the coast and rises toward the interior. On entering the continent, the explorer must cut his way through swamps of mangrove-trees in order to reach the table-lands, the hills, the mountains, the plain.

We have learned more within the last eighty-five years of the geography of Africa than people knew in the preceding eighteen centuries. Strictly speaking, Mungo Park is the father of African exploration. True, the enterprising Phœnicians sent out colonies to the "Dark Continent," and the warlike Greeks made conquests there. The Roman standards were also unfurled on African soil; but so far as we know these nations confined their operations to the coasts of the Red Sea, the Mediterranean, and Egypt. They did not penetrate the interior. The Carthaginians claim to have sent their merchants into the Niger valley, but there is no evidence to support this boast. It was reserved for the nineteenth century civilization to open Africa to the gaze of the world.

In 1788, "The African Association" was formed in England, for the purpose of exploring "Inner Africa." They sent out Mungo Park, whose great career as an explorer inspired Barth, Overweg, Livingstone, Stanley, and De Brazza, and led them to achieve a work for Africa for which humanity will ever be grateful, and upon which God will forever pour out His heavenly benedictions.

I can not in a paragraph, or even a page, follow the history of African exploration, or describe the physical features and peculiarities of this interesting country. The reader will find agreeable and profitable work in studying, in the latest geographies, the coast lines, the rivers, the lakes, the snow-clad mountains, the deserts, and the swamps of Africa. Such a study will not fail to produce surprise, because we, who passed through the schools a generation ago, are so ignorant of the topography and physical conformations of the Dark Continent. We think of it simply as a horrid, sickly country. We can hardly believe that within it are snow-clad mountains, charming valleys, and lovely landscape scenery.

Africa is a beautiful country. Let the reader imagine

THE BASSA COUNTRY COAST.

himself viewing the land from the deck of a steamer. The golden-sanded beach stretches away into the distance. The waves look like crystal drops as they break amidst the golden sands. From amidst the dense, variegated foliage come the sweet carolings of birds of beautiful plumage. Back of all are the everlasting hills, standing at some points on the coast like grand old sentinels of nature. Beyond them all are the mountain ranges, seen dimly through the eyes, but rising boldly in your glasses. The water of ocean, lake, and river is clear as crystal—beautiful as a sea of glass. The azure skies glisten in the light of the sun, but grow soft when "the stars hold their vigil around the midnight throne." It is grand. I saw it and rejoiced.

Our steamer stopped in the harbor of a West African city. A small boat came for me from the shore. I descended the ladder, crossed the dangerous sand-bar, and stood early one August morning upon African soil. It was in the confines of the Americo-African Republic, known in the family of nations as Liberia; where colored Americans have been going for more than half a century with the hope to find a field in which to grow to the full stature of manhood, and to exercise the prerogatives of rulers in a government of Africans.

Monrovia, built on a plateau including an area of about three-quarters of a mile square, eighty feet above the level of the sea, on the summit of Cape Mesurado, the Plymouth Rock of Liberia, looks picturesque. The whole view is charming. Here, sixty-five years ago, a band of brave, heroic colored people from America landed and established a home of their own. Here, thirty-eight years ago, a government of the Negro, for the Negro, and by the Negro was instituted, amidst praise and prayer. Sharp and uneven has been the contest. Poor and unlettered men have struggled with "the audacity of faith" to solve the Problem of Negro Independence. Various have been the opposing forces. Death has reaped an abundant harvest. War, hunger, and disease have been his instruments. The struggle still continues, but with no apparent decisive results. Interesting is the impression which I formed of this country—its climate, resources, and people.

CHAPTER II.

THE SEARCH FOR AFRICAN TERRITORY.

THE Americo-African Republic is situated on the western shore of Africa, occupying what is known as the Grain Coast. Its undisputed territory begins on the north, from the south bank of the Manna River, about 6° 80′ north latitude, and runs as far south as the San Pedro River, about 4° 20′ north latitude, a distance of about 600 miles. Its interior boundary can not be definitely stated. Some authorities make it to run back about 200 miles. East of Liberia is the Soudan, the abode of Ethiopia's teeming millions; on the west is the Atlantic Ocean; north is Sierra Leone, the English colony; and south, though not contiguous, is Ashantee, the powerful Negro monarchy.

Running down the West Coast we come to a French possession, Grand Bassam; and next, the English colonies, Axim and Cape Coast. The English desire to secure Grand Bassam from the French. If they succeed, either by purchase or seizure, the entire coast line from Sierra Leone to the Cameroons would be under the control of an English-speaking people, and under the influence of British and Americo-African civilization. This would include a coast line of about two thousand geographical miles.

Liberia is the fruit of American colonization. The first practical colonizationist was a Negro, Paul Cuffee, of New Bedford, Mass. This bold leader, full of zeal for the civilization of Africa, took, in 1815, forty colored persons in his own vessel, at his own expense, from Boston to Sierra Leone, which was the colony established on the West African Coast by Great Britain for the reception of slaves captured from the Americans in the Revolutionary War.

Rev. Dr. G. W. Samson, ex-President of Columbian University, Washington, D. C., in a Memorial on behalf of Liberian Interests, presented to the President of the United States, and to the Secretary of State, September 18, 1885, makes this historically accurate statement:

"Liberia had its origin in a want and duty of the United States. That want is presented in the Constitution of the United States, Art. I., Sec. 9, Par. 1, in these words: 'The migration or importation of such persons as any of the States now existing shall think proper to admit, shall not be prohibited by the Congress prior to the year one thousand eight hundred and eight.'

"This period expired near the close of the second term of President Jefferson's administration. Being recognized as referring mainly to the importation of slaves from Africa, President Jefferson considered the need of an asylum for Africans to be seized and provided for when expected violations of law should occur. His first suggestion was a treaty with Great Britain, which Power had transferred African slaves, taken during the war for American Independence, to Sierra Leone; permitting that colony to serve as the asylum required. The second war with Great Britain, under President Madison, frustrated this design and deferred the provision needed.

"Under President Monroe the necessity for such an asylum became imperative, since captured slaves could not be protected when returned to the African Coast."

Congress was petitioned to establish a colony on the West Coast of Africa, and responded favorably with a report containing the recommendation, that stipulations be obtained from Great Britain and other maritime powers, both for the suppression of the slave-trade, and also "*guaranteeing a permanent neutrality for any colony of free people of color, which, at the expense and under the auspices of the United States, shall be established on the African Coast*"; to which was added:

Resolved, That adequate provision be hereafter made to defray any necessary expenses which may be incurred in carrying the preceding resolution into effect.

Finally, on the 3d of March, 1819, an Act was passed by Congress, authorizing the President (then President Monroe) to return all recaptured Africans to Africa, and to provide for their support by establishing an Agency on the West Coast.

The Colonization Society, which was organized in 1816, having as officers such men as Henry Clay, Bushrod Washington, and President Monroe, became, practically, the General Agent of the United States, carrying out the provision of the Act of 1819 in the selection and establishment of what is now known as the Republic of Liberia. Practically this was a Government venture—the only colonial enterprise to which this country ever committed itself.

In February, 1820, Samuel Bacon, as United States Agent, started from New York City for the West Coast of Africa with eighty-eight persons of color, in the ship *Elizabeth*, which was chartered by the Government, and sailed under the flag of the United States. The colored colonists were given free passage, they agreeing to prepare suitable accommodations on the West Coast for the recaptured Africans.

The colonists made their first stop, after leaving New York City, at Freetown, the capital of the English colony, Sierra Leone. Thence they sailed to the island of Sherbro, where they disembarked. The English governor gave the Americans permission to reside there until a location on the mainland of Africa could be chosen and purchased.

It was very unhealthy at Sherbro. It is so now. Fever made sad havoc. Death was busy. The grave was never closed. Back to Sierra Leone, from the jaws of death, the disheartened remnant fled. Many died there. In Fourah Bay they laid them down to rest till the trump of the archangel and the voice of God shall proclaim the dissolution of the earth and the resurrection of the dead. Great were the difficulties experienced in planting this American colony; but the Government and the Society kept straight onward.

In October, 1821, the United States Government ordered Lieut. R. F. Stockton, of the Navy, to proceed to the West Coast of Africa, and select and purchase territory for the United States Agency.

Stopping at Sierra Leone, Lieut. Stockton's war-vessel took on board the Agent and a few of the colored American colonists. They moved slowly down the coast, looking for an inviting site for the settlement. When they came to Cape Mesurado,* a bold promontory, eighty feet above the level of the sea, the party decided to make a purchase of land. The war-ship hove-to and dropped anchor. The Lieutenant (who was promoted to be Captain, and who subsequently became Commodore) went ashore. He explored the country round about the lofty Cape, rowing up the Mesurado River, and a stream which now bears the name of this bold and brave officer—Stockton Creek.

While Capt. Stockton and his party moved around by day, interviewing the native kings and chiefs, and examining and exploring the country, the slave-traders were also at work. They knew that a settlement there would destroy their business.

A foreign-born colored man in their employ circulated among the natives lies and slanders prejudicial to the Americans. The aboriginal kings and chiefs were made to feel that Capt. Stockton's enterprise meant no good to them, but would prove positively hurtful. They were urged to refuse to sell any part of the land to the American people.

Of course there was arranged a public conference. The Africans call it "Palaver." The day came. The King and Chiefs assembled with scores of their armed followers. Capt. Stockton and escort, Agent Eli Ayres, and a few colored American colonists were on hand; so was the colored slave-trader.

The "Palaver" began. Capt. Stockton explained his

---

* This Cape was named by the Spaniards. In the early days of the slave-trade a squad of well-armed Spanish marines landed there, searching doubtless for slaves. The natives attacked them. A furious contest took place, and the Spaniards were cut down by the bold, warlike Deys. During the fight, the Spanish marines cried " Misericordia ! Misericordia !" "Mercy ! Mercy !" The Cape came to be called Mesurado ; by some, Montserrado, a corruption of the Spanish " Misericordia."

mission, and made his proposal for the purchase of land The natives replied. The "Palaver" grew warm. The colored slave-trader, who could speak the native language, the Dey, boldly and frequently interjected such comments and interruptions as were clearly making trouble. Feeling ran high. Imminent peril threatened the lives of the Americans. Destruction would have overtaken the strangers, had not Capt. Stockton, with great coolness and presence of mind, drawn his revolver, held it at the colored slave-trader's head, ordered his marines to prepare to fire, and threatened death to any man who dared to break the peace. Under this self-possessed and determined action the colored slave-trader grew "mild as a sucking dove." The natives, knowing the white man's war power, and seeing "the fighting ship" in the harbor, grew calm, and the negotiations proceeded decently and in order. The result was the signing and delivery of this deed of sale:

"Witnesseth: That whereas certain persons, citizens of the United States of America, are desirous to establish themselves on the Western Coast of Africa, and have invested Capt. Robert F. Stockton and Eli Ayres with full powers to treat with and purchase from us, the said kings, princes, and head men, certain lands [which are described], we do hereby, in consideration of [certain specified articles or merchandise], forever cede and relinquish the above described lands to Capt. Robert F. Stockton and Eli Ayres; To Have and To Hold the said premises for the use of these said citizens of America."

This deed was duly executed and delivered on payment of the stipulated price by these Agents of the United States Government, and thus was planted the seed of what has grown to be the Americo-African Republic.

CHAPTER III

THE STRUGGLE TO ESTABLISH THE COLONY.

IT is not my purpose to dwell upon the details of Liberian history. Therefore with this brief statement, which should not be overlooked, and which will interest the reader, I shall pass to an examination of the climate, resources, and people of the country.

The slave-traders were not easily subdued. They were cast down, but not destroyed. They were vanquished, but not routed. They lingered around the Cape, stirred up the bad blood of the natives, and incited them to make war on the colonists.

Soon after the purchase, which Capt. Stockton effected, a large number of armed natives made their appearance and attacked the colonists. They were driven away; but for months they annoyed the new settlers, causing them to sleep on their arms, and to build their cabins with their swords at their sides and their guns within reach.

It was a time that tried men's souls. These difficulties alone caused great hardships; but they were not all. An enemy more persistent than the hostile natives, and deadlier by far, played sad havoc in that heroic colony.

The West Coast of Africa is called "The White Man's Grave." Mr. Spurgeon, the great London divine, said to me in April, 1883: "We English people think the West Coast climate fatal to white men. We always have two Governors for our colony, Sierra Leone—one dead, being brought home; and the other alive, on his way out."

The spirit of this remark is true. White men can not stand the climate. After a bitter struggle with it they either retire or die. Missionaries, traders, and commercial men go to the West Coast with the understanding, which is usually put in the contract, that they must have a change of climate in two or three years. There are the exceptions; but the rule for white men is to retire or die.

This fact tried both the Government and their General Agent, the Colonization Society, in their early efforts to foster the colony planted in 1821 at Cape Mesurado, where now stands Monrovia, the capital of Liberia, named in honor of President Monroe.

As early as 1822 there was not a white American on the Cape. The hostile climate put to flight even the intrepid Dr. Eli Ayres. It would have destroyed Liberia, root and branch, had it not been for the heroic conduct of one of the noblest men the world has ever seen. He was a Negro. His son, born in Africa, an Americo-African, is now the able and scholarly President of the Republic of Liberia.

The name of ELIJAH JOHNSON is held in great reverence by all of his countrymen. Like Toussaint L'Ouverture he was brave and heroic; and like George Washington he was patriotic and noble. When, under the pressure of the hostile natives and a deadly climate, it was proposed to abandon the settlement on Cape Mesurado and return to the United States, Elijah Johnson lifted up his voice and made this heroic declaration: "I have been two years searching for a home in Africa. I have found it; and *I shall stay here.*"

This courageous stand touched the hearts of the people; and they resolved to establish right there a home and a government for themselves, their posterity, and their brethren who were still in bondage in America, or to die in the attempt. The white agents, thoroughly discouraged, abandoned the enterprise, and Elijah Johnson became Governor of the colony.

The situation was gloomy. None but a hero could have faced it undaunted. The climate was trying. The natives were exceedingly hostile. They regretted the sale of the Cape, and determined to expel or exterminate the colonists. Governor Johnson's naval stores became exhausted. Who can fitly describe the embarrassing situation? The Governor and his followers must have felt like the American Pilgrim Fathers when, with bated breath, they said one to the other, "Our supplies are out"! Here, it was death from wild Indians, starvation, and cold on Plymouth Rock. There, it was death from hostile Africans, fever, and exposure on Cape Mesurado. But annihilation was only threatened. It did not come. God sent the ship with daily bread to the American Rock; and He too sent the ship with naval stores to the African Cape.

One night the sentry hearing a noise not far from the settlement and thinking that the natives were approaching, fired a cannon, and aroused the sleeping colonists. There was, however, no cause for alarm. The noise may have been caused by the footsteps of some prowling leopards; but there was a special Providence in the firing of that cannon.

An English man-of-war was passing. Hearing the discharge, the commander dropped anchor and sent a detail ashore to make an investigation. The colonists rejoiced at this opportunity to supply themselves with powder. They were even then recognized as an ally in the suppression of the slave-trade.

Again Governor Johnson saved a country and a Government to his posterity. The English naval officer volunteered assistance by arms and effective protection if a few feet of ground were ceded on which to erect the British flag. Gov. Johnson promptly replied, "We want no flag-staff put up here that will cost more to get it down than to whip the natives." In this patriotic act Elijah Johnson showed that he possessed the mind and the spirit of a far-seeing statesman. He looked down the vista of coming ages and saw the occurrences of the present generation, the scramble for West African territory which is going on among European nations. Had England planted herself then on Cape Mesurado, she never would have withdrawn.

But, as our aim is not history, we pass over the events of Gov. Johnson's administration. We shall not pause to describe the growth and development of the colony under the fostering care of the American Colonization Society; nor the heroic and self-sacrificing labors of such men as Governors Ayres, Ashmun, Russwurm, Pinney, and Lot Cary. It is enough now and here to say that the early American settlers in Africa met and bore their difficulties with a brave and heroic spirit, finding their greatest obstacle in a trying, a hostile, a deadly climate.

CHAPTER IV.

CLIMATE—THE RAINY SEASON.

THE Americo-African Republic lies wholly within the tropics, and is very near the equator. Its southern extremity is only four degrees north of that great belt, and its northern limit seven degrees. The days and nights are practically equal. There is no twilight. Darkness follows fast behind the setting sun; and the daylight breaks again suddenly upon the darkness.

The climate is essentially different from that of the United States, excepting the lower part of Florida. Perpetual summer reigns. The grass and foliage are ever green.

But torrid heat does not always prevail. Indeed the new-comer is generally surprised by the prevailing climate of the West Coast. We usually think of Africa as a red-hot furnace. True, in Nubia and Upper Egypt eggs may be roasted in the hot sand; but along the Mediterranean and to the south of the Desert of Sahara the climate is more temperate; at times cold. Indeed, in the interior and even near the equator perpetual snow is found.

The West African year may be divided into two seasons, the wet and the dry. The rain begins in Liberia in May, and ceases in October. It is dry the remainder of the year.

This is the recognized division; but in some respects it is confusing. It is impossible to accurately define these seasons. An English sea-captain of thirty years' experience on the West Coast, tried to give a description to his friends, but failed. He impatiently said, "This is the idea; In the rainy season it rains every day, and in the dry season it rains any day." But this is not true.

In the rainy season there are some beautiful days. Many an afternoon have I enjoyed a boat-ride on the Monrovia Bay in this season. It has rained in the Dries as if the clouds were all falling down upon the earth. In the rainy season there is what is called the Middle Dries. For from three to six weeks Nature gives man an opportunity to gather in his rice crop. She will not starve him, if he is industrious. The sky is clear; the sun shines bright;

the air is cool and bracing. After long, weary months of water, mud, and dampness, the Middle Dries brings sunshine, vigor, and cheerfulness. One feels as if he could live forever in such a climate; but it ends; and the rains begin again with increased fury, as if to make up for lost time. They call it Middle Dries because it comes between the seasons—in the middle of them. It is clear from all this, that there can be no arbitrary division of the year.

Terrific tornadoes precede and end the rainy season. In April and October the skies resound with the clash of electric shocks. The forked lightning leaps and dances through the clouds, the forests, and the earth; and the winds howl furiously or moan piteously.

By May everybody is prepared for the rains, just as in the Northern part of the United States people are ready by Thanksgiving Day for winter; and when they fairly get to falling, the man who sees them for the first time, wonders if the world is again to be destroyed by a flood, and if the great day of the Lord has come.

Rising one morning in August off the West Coast, I looked through the port of our steamer and was surprised at the thickness of what appeared to be a fog. I dressed and started on deck for a walk before breakfast. To my surprise I found that we were in the African rains. It was like a fog on Long Island Sound, or off the coasts of Newfoundland. At times our steamer stood still, the pilot being unable to find his way through the drenching, driving rain.

The prevailing weather during this season is damp and cool. The thermometer averages 70° Fahrenheit. A fire is comfortable in the early morning and in the evening. Indeed, the natives, at dark, invariably build fires in their houses, and keep them up all night. This is healthy and wise. The Americo-Africans do not have a fire in their houses. Most of the houses are built in style like those in the Southern part of the United States. The kitchen is off from the house; and in Liberia the residences, as a rule, are without fire-places. Dampness, therefore, reigns supreme. My towels have hung on the wash-stand rack in my bedroom damp from one day to another. No wonder that rheumatism is a common complaint among the Americo-Africans.

The stranger is comfortable in the rainy season in the same clothing which is worn in New York or London in the fall of the year, excepting the overcoat. Much of the suffering among the emigrants sent out by the American Colonization Society arises from the fact that they go to the West Coast from "the sweet, sunny South," without sufficient or proper clothing. Flannel ought to be worn next to the skin, and most persons who can afford it, do so. Although there are many who advocate cotton as undergarments; yet, all other things being equal, those wearing flannel are healthier than those who wear cotton, often nothing at all, underneath their outer clothing.

There is less sickness and there are fewer deaths in the rainy than in the dry season. Body and mind have more vigor. The evenings remind us of the long American winter nights, when we close the blinds, pull down the curtains, stir up the fire, light the gas, draw up to the study table, and commune with those gifted and immortal minds who have left "footprints on the sands of time."

In this season business slackens. The rivers rise and become dangerous. Travel on them is often attended with fatal consequences. The Government of Liberia has done comparatively nothing for internal improvements, such as opening roads, building bridges, etc.; hence it is impossible to move around through the country freely during the rains. The merchants and traders sit quietly in their places of business, review the transactions of the last dry season, and plan their operations for the next. The camwood and palm-trees, which furnish valuable articles of trade, grow on undisturbed even by native industry. The coffee-tree and sugar-cane, the chief staples of Liberian agriculture, enlarge, and blossom, and mature, while the cultivators lounge and cry, like the old Southern slave, " More rain, more rest."

It is impossible to give a clear idea of the African rains. The water does not fall in drops, but in sheets. It sounds as if all the clouds were tumbling down at once. If the reader should take a hogshead of water to the third story window of a house and empty it upon the roof of the piazza below, he would have an idea of how the falling rain sounded in Africa to me, as I listened to it under the iron roof of my attic room.

But the gloom, and the damp, and the rain, and the wind, like all things human, change ; and we come out of them into the bright, cheering sunlight.

CHAPTER V.

CLIMATE—THE DRY SEASON.

OCTOBER is the month of light tornadoes and frequent showers. It is, therefore, called " the month of short journeys." It ushers in the dry season. With it " the melancholy days" depart and the bright skies are, as a rule, without a cloud.

These African tornadoes are wondrous to behold. They

come suddenly, and for a brief space of time riot madly, and as suddenly end their fury.

One afternoon I was boat-riding with some friends on Monrovia Bay. Suddenly a cloud, "no bigger than a man's hand," appeared. Rapidly it spread over the heavens until it cast deep darkness upon the waters. We headed for the land; and our Kroo boatmen pulled hard for the shore. The bay became suddenly turbulent. We were dashed hither and thither by the white-crested waves. The wind grew fiercer every moment. The black clouds completely blotted out the sun. The lightning flashes became blinding and rapid. The heavens, at times, for a brief moment seemed to be on fire. The thunder roared like hungry lions eager for their prey. Man and bird and beast rushed pell-mell to seek shelter from the storm. Suddenly the lightning ceased; the thunder hushed; and the winds died away. Then as suddenly the rain descended in torrents and the floods came with the voice of many waters. In an hour or two it was all over; and the silvery moon shone with great splendor.

November is the queen of the months. The dome of heaven is beautiful beyond description. The grass is greener after the rains. Everything is brighter for the washing. Out of the thick, variegated foliage a rosebud, a blossom, or a flower peeps; and lo! the sweet notes of birds of beautiful plumage are heard. Even the stranger, worn with fever, wonders why this is not considered the loveliest climate on the face of the earth. I have plunged into the ocean surf in the early morning; and in the afternoon I have wandered up the hill and along " the shores of the far-resounding sea," till the setting sun went down with my messages of cheer, which I invariably sent to my friends across the boundless deep.

I have never seen more beautiful days than those of November and December in Liberia. The azure skies, the golden beams of the sun, the fragrance of the early morning, and the cool breezes of the afternoon, all unite to make the heart rejoice and the soul to praise God. I was once in an interior Liberian town, Arthington, bosomed in green and lofty hills, at whose feet the St. Paul's River flows making sweet music as it madly leaps and dashes over the murmuring shallows. I looked from my window over the hills and valleys and saw a brilliant sunrise, and felt the full force of Addison's sublime ode:

> The unwearied sun from day to day
> Doth his Creator's power display,
> And publishes to every land
> The work of an almighty hand.

But it is the night scene I most admired. One sees brilliancy beyond description when

> "The stars hold their vigil round the midnight throne."

The clearness of the atmosphere can not be excelled by anything of the kind which is known in other parts of the world. Famous as is the Italian sky, I think it can hardly rival what one sees in Africa. European astronomers, it is said, visiting this land, especially in the midst of the Dries, look with astonishment on the nocturnal splendor of the heavens; some of the planets shining with great brilliancy and occasioning deep and well-defined shadows.

The thermometer in this season shows an average, until the month of February, of about 85° Fahrenheit. It would be too high to put it at 90°. It never is as hot as in New York City in mid-summer. Most people are surprised at this. Nevertheless it is true that Americans experience hotter weather in August, especially in the centres of civilization, than the Liberians ever feel.

What a strange world! In November the people of the United States are having cold weather. The merchants sell their "Fall and Winter goods." I was in a large mercantile establishment in Liberia early in December, and was surprised to see upon the counters and shelves "Spring and Summer goods"—bright calicoes, straw hats and bonnets, white vests, linen coats, etc., etc.

About the middle of December a cold, disagreeable, and dangerous wind blows through the land. It is like the sirocco that sweeps over Italy. It is called the "Harmattan Wind." It blows for from four to six weeks. During these winds the thermometer at sunrise and at sunset averages 66°, and it seldom rises higher than 80° at any time during the day.

The Harmattan comes from the interior; some say from the Desert of Sahara. It injures vegetation, and affects the lower animals. Man does not escape. It is the sickly season. Deaths are frequent. People suffer from neuralgia, colds, and coughs; and even the natives are affected. The Harmattan is no respecter of persons. It dries up the eyes, nostrils, and mouth; chaps the lips, the hands, and the face; opens the seams of furniture, and curls up the leaves of books just as the heat of the fire would do. Indeed, it plays havoc in general with man and beast. The physicians and druggists, though few in number, keep busy, and the undertaker and the grave-digger are not unemployed.

All this was a surprise in my experience. When getting my medicines in London, I struck Ayer's Cherry Pectoral from the list. What would I want with a remedy for colds and coughs on the West Coast of Africa? A cold was my first complaint!

After the Harmattan, until the rains again, hot weather holds high carnival. February and March are the hottest months of the year. They are also the sickliest. The thermometer, it is said, keeps above the nineties, though it rarely exceeds 95°; but the heat is intense, and the sea breeze, which blows from about ten o'clock in the morning until midnight, does not suffice to moisten the dry and oppressive atmosphere.

By this time the reader, doubtless, asks, why is there so much said about "the trying African climate"? What an equable temperature seems to prevail! No part of the United States can match it. For about six months there is an average of 72°; for about three months it is from 85° to 90°; and at no time does the thermometer stay for any length of time above 95°. Why is not this considered as lovely a climate as is found anywhere on the earth?

We answer, it would be a delightful climate, a healthy country, a veritable El Dorado, if it were not for this fact —*Malaria is king!*

CHAPTER VI.

CLIMATE—CAUSES OF UNHEALTHINESS.

THE Americo-African Republic, like Holland, has a low and flat coast. Marshes and swamps of mangrove-trees abound. These trees thrive in mud. They are found near the mouths of rivers, and form a close and impenetrable thicket. They spread rapidly, propagating themselves. Their branches turn down, seek the mud, and grow to be trees, and in this way increase and perpetuate the species. Their foliage is abundant and dense, forming secure retreats for multitudes of aquatic birds. The leaves and branches of these trees fall and rot and form a sickening mass of decayed vegetation. In the dry season, particularly, the sun brings out of this reeking bed of putrefaction an extraordinary amount of poison that mingles with the air, and both man and beast inhale disease and receive the seeds of infirmity or death.

These swamps, and their sickly, deadly condition, give character to the climate of the entire West Coast belt, which extends back into the country for several miles. It is hard to fix a definite limit. It varies at different points, following the physical conformations of the country. This malarial coast belt is the greatest barrier in the way of the growth and development of the Americo-African Republic. As long as the swamps and marshes stand; as long as there is not money or energy enough to counteract, to some extent, by drainage, sewerage, and other modern appliances, the effect of these miasmas, so long will Malaria reign!

Dr. Edward W. Blyden, a Negro of great learning, who has lived since 1852 on the West Coast of Africa, says, in a scholarly paper in an English magazine:*

"Now it is well known that a belt of malarious lands, which are hot-beds of fever, extends along the whole of the West Coast of Africa, running from forty to fifty miles back from the sea-coast. In this region of country neither horses nor cattle will thrive. Horses will not live at all. Sheep, goats, and hogs drag out an indifferent existence. At Sierra Leone, Monrovia, and other settlements on the coast, fortunes have been expended by lovers of horses in trying to keep them, but with the most scrupulous and expensive care they die.

"The interior tribes, who have from time to time migrated to the coast, have perished or degenerated. Every child born on the coast is stunted, physically and mentally,

---

* *Fraser's Magazine*, October, 1876.

in the cradle by the jungle fever which assails it a few days after birth. European infants seldom survive such attacks. The very tribe occupying the country about Gallinas and Cape Mount have traditions that they came to the coast as conquerors, driving before them all tribal organizations which opposed their march. They were a numerous, intelligent, handsome people. Now only melancholy traces of what they once were can be discovered in individuals of that waning tribe.

"As long as the malarious vegetation and deadly mangrove swamps occupy so large a portion of West African territory, there will be no more probability of making any permanent moral or even material progress on the coast, or of developing a great mind, than there is in improving the haunts of the polar bear and the reindeer."

Being a pure Negro, and an enthusiastic advocate of the colonization of American colored people on the West Coast, and also a resident of Africa for nearly thirty-five years, Dr. Blyden's view of the climate may be accepted as sound and correct.

I have seen both cows and horses on the West Coast; but they were small and spiritless. They were living at "a poor dying rate." The English Governor of Sierra Leone keeps a horse, but he would not be able to sell it in London. Nobody would own the poor, cadaverous-looking creature. I have ridden horseback in Monrovia; but though brought down from the interior about eighty miles, the animal was small and spiritless. Under the depressing influence of the coast climate he became worthless in a month, and soon died. Indeed, the life of man and beast on the coast has been described by Dr. Blyden in these words; which he applies only to white men, but which admit of general application:

"The miasma seems to have a singular effect; .... where it does not at once extinguish life, it diminishes imperceptibly its force, sapping physical energy and rendering the mind dull and spiritless." *

Rev. Dr. Wilson, who from long years of residence and travel in West Africa, knew the climate well, and whose book, "Western Africa," breathes a Christian, an unprejudiced, and a hopeful spirit, says:

"A belt of the densest wood and jungle of a hundred miles wide, extends along the whole length of Western Africa, and is, no doubt, the chief cause of the sickness which prevails in this region. .... When these natural forests are once cut down, the land is soon covered by a jungle of undergrowth which is almost impenetrable for man or beast." † He also says:

"Another great drawback to the prosperity of Liberia is the undoubted unhealthiness of the climate. The process of acclimation must be passed through even by colored persons; and for the first six months it is quite as trying to them as to the whites." ‡

Another writer may be profitably quoted in this connection. He says: "The sun pours its fiercest rays upon these marshes. They become stagnant, and the vegetable and animal matter in them becomes putrid. The breeze passes over these desolate and extensive regions and carries with it the seeds of fever and death in every direction." §

Finally, let us get the testimony of one of the United States Ministers to the Republic of Liberia. He wrote the Government: "It has been demonstrated that neither horses nor mules can withstand the climate on the sea-coast.

---

* "From West Africa to Palestine," p. 15.   † "Western Africa," p. 27.
‡ Ibid., p. 104.   § Moister's "Memorials of Missionary Labors in Africa."

2*

Horses are found in the interior, but when brought to the coast they sicken and die. Although constant summer prevails, as to temperature, the miasmatic influence caused by heavy rains alternating with the hot sunshine, causes sickness during six months of the year, and during the remaining six months the power of the sun is such that it is almost impossible for any one, except a native, to work; as it produces inertia, lassitude, want of energy. Indeed, after a man has once had the fever he never, in Africa, regains the energy he was possessed of before."*

This is a strong statement. I do not indorse it in its entirety. Its general tendency is correct. Perhaps, however, we have tarried here too long. Everybody believes the climate to be unhealthy; but everybody is not informed as to the nature and extent of the unhealthiness. Many turn their backs upon the West Coast of Africa, with the sneer, "It's a death-trap"; while others either conceal or deny the unhealthiness of its coast-belt. Let us enter our earnest protest against both positions. Back from the Liberian coast, for example, are the hills, the Finley and the Kong Mountains, a salubrious climate and a healthy land; and this is also true of the Congo. But capital, brains, and energy are required to open wagon-roads, build bridges, construct railroads, put freight boats on the rivers, and thus flood the country with the appliances of modern civilization. I know that civilization is a thing of slow growth; but changes from barbarism to enlightenment are so rapid in these days that it would not be extravagant to picture a wonderful growth in African commerce and civilization if easy access to the interior lands were made by means of wagon and rail roads and boat facilities. The ob-

---

* Dispatch, No. 273, of the Legation of the United States, dated Monrovia, Liberia, Sept. 3d, 1877.

stacles arising out of the blighting malarial swamps of the African coast may be overcome, as in other countries, by the investment of capital, and by drainage and sewerage.

CHAPTER VII.

CLIMATE—MALARIA DETHRONED.

THE Americo-African Republic is not alone in its struggles against a swampy coast-belt. Holland's coast lands have always been hot-beds of malarial diseases, of fever and death. I learned in the land of the Dutch that an army officer, when transferred from Amsterdam to Rotterdam, on the coast, suffers from malarial fever Any traveller who makes observations on the low, marshy coasts of Holland, goes away fully impressed with the belief that they must be the home of diseases and periodical fevers. The excessive mortality among English armies in the Netherlands is not to be wondered at. That they died like sheep was perfectly natural.*

The sea-coast of the Southern States of the United States was exceedingly malarial; until, at the inhabited points, engineering, drainage, and general sanitary appliances counteracted or destroyed the effect of the deadly poison. From Virginia to Florida thousands of the pioneer settlers fell victims to the malaria of the American coast; but they pushed back into the country; and wherever they built cities, they brought capital to their rescue

---

* See Sir John Pringle's Observations.

in counteracting the poison arising from the low, flat lands upon which they built. There is a parallel between the Settlement of Delaware and African colonization.

My native city, Charleston, S. C., is fifty per cent. healthier than it was a half century ago. Money and science have dethroned malaria. So will it be on the West Coast of Africa. Interior cities of commercial activity, a farming country of systematic industry will come into existence in response to the influence of our Christian civilization; and then the cities on the coast, through which there must be ingress and egress both of population and commodities, will be able to command capital to at least moderate the malarial effects of the swampy surroundings.

It is somewhat healthier now at points on the African coast than it was fifty years ago. At Freetown, the capital of Sierra Leone, and at Monrovia, the capital of Liberia, the stranger talks of the blessings of health, when he hears the sickening accounts of the mortality of the last generation. The unhealthiness of the Congo will be greatly modified as capital and the appliances of modern civilization enter the country.

But while all this is true, I have no patience with those who underrate the effect of the climate of the West Coast of Africa upon colonizers from America or Europe. It is a crime to conceal from a man who turns his face to Africa, the fact that those swamps and marshes will prove an annoying, a trying, perhaps a fatal enemy; that in his battle for life and struggle for bread, malaria will possibly cripple him by robbing him of energy and spirit. Let him know this, so that forewarned, he may be forearmed.

I have not looked favorably on schemes to colonize any part of Africa with the poor and the comparatively ignorant masses of Europe or America. What can men, without means, without any knowledge of practical hygiene or of sanitary requirements, do in the presence of malaria, intrenched as it is in the swamps of the African coast? If, in addition to this, they emigrate with the idea of having an easy time, of finding bread growing on trees, of gathering where they do not sow, as the masses of colonizers too often do, they must fail in their hopes and expectations ; for the malarial atmosphere will unfit them for the struggle which awaits every one who goes to a new country; and their poverty and inexperience and physical indisposition will keep them in helplessness amidst their swampy surroundings.

Let hardy, energetic, and determined people, especially those of African blood, go from the American States or the British colonies fully informed as to the conditions of life in Africa ; let capital be judiciously invested, first in subjecting the malarial swamps at chosen points to sanitary and hygienic appliances ; and, secondly, to the opening of roads and the planting of interior settlements; and the whole world would profit in the rapid increase of commerce, and the steady advancement of civilization, and the gradual spread of Christianity.

There must, of course, be seaport towns and cities. But in the development of West African interests, on the Congo, on the Niger, in Liberia, the interior people and settlements will be the backbone of the country. The mountaineers of every land are noted for their sterling qualities. The atmosphere of the country and of the highlands makes a stalwart manhood.

Fifteen miles back from the Atlantic Ocean, I stood on a range of hills in Liberia, and looked down upon the waters of the sea. The people of this locality, on the St.

Paul's River, are healthier than the Monrovians, whose home is on the coast. I went still further back, and found it growing healthier as I journeyed toward the interior.

At Arthington, the most flourishing settlement in Liberia, only thirty miles from the coast, I found myself in an exceedingly hilly country, with a somewhat salubrious climate, and a hardy people living in comparative comfort. The children were not delicate, and puny, and full of sores as those on the coast; but they were fleshy, chubby, and full of life. One pities most of the Americo-African coast children. He feels like romping on the grass with those of a place like Arthington. Almost everything calls forth the stranger's wonder and admiration. What strikes him as the most hopeful and encouraging sign is the fact that thousands of acres are already under cultivation, and there is a small increase steadily going on in the quantity of land which is planted.

It is work done back from the coast, or which leads civilizing influences into the interior, that will do for Africa what commerce, philanthropy, and Christianity wish to perform. Good roads with substantial bridges must be constructed, and communication opened up between the people of the African mountains and their fellow-countrymen on the coast, who are in direct contact with the civilized world. And who would dare to foretell the results of such a course? Who can foresee the effect upon the hardy, progressive natives whose *habitat* is beyond the malarious belt of the deadly coast climate? And would not the colored Americans grasp the opportunities that such contact with Africa would produce? Who can tell what a mighty commerce and what a powerful civilization would grow up where such deep and broad foundations already exist? For we are told that many of the interior

MONROVIA, THE CAPITAL OF LIBERIA.

natives are practicing some of the most important industries of life, maintaining schools, and living in comparative comfort and peace. Both Mungo Park and Barth record in their explorations the fact that in the heart of Africa they found well-cultivated fields, weaving, dyeing, smithing, markets, and armies. Mungo Park said of Sego, the capital of Bambara: "The view of this extensive city, the numerous canoes upon the river, the crowded population, and the cultivated state of the surrounding country, formed altogether a prospect of civilization and magnificence which I little expected to find in the bosom of Africa."[*]

Let capital and science counteract malaria on the coast and turn the stream of civilization towards the interior, and mighty results will follow all worthy efforts to develop the country, and to civilize the people.

CHAPTER VIII.

CLIMATE—AFRICAN FEVER.

THE African coast climate is spoken of as unhealthy by many people who do not know what special form of complaint manifests itself there. Europeans and Americans suffer from malarial troubles, fever and ague. It is simply this, and nothing more, that afflicts the emigrants to Africa, and even the natives who inhabit the coast-belt. The disorders and symptoms may be greater in Liberia and Congo than in New Orleans or Arkansas; but it is a matter of degree, not of kind.

On the West Coast this malarial complaint is called

---

[*] Travels, Chap. II.

"African fever." It is no respecter of persons. It attacks everybody. The greatest explorers, the wealthiest merchants, and the most devoted missionaries have succumbed to its ravages. Sometimes it attacks a new-comer on his arrival. Then there are people who go to Africa and live for months without any symptoms of fever; but it never fails to lay siege to the unacclimated system.

The nature of the attack depends upon circumstances. The constitution and physical condition, the quality of the food and the state of the mind, all enter into the process of acclimation. If a person goes to the West Coast with a good constitution in healthy condition, free from hereditary or acquired weaknesses or diseases; if he can get there wholesome food to eat, not depending wholly upon the diet of the country; if he is so circumstanced as to be free from special mental burdens or anxieties, being contented, cheerful, and happy, he may have no fear of the African fever. He will easily acclimate. But if these conditions be reversed, then the person either dies a victim of fever, as hundreds before him, or he loses his vigor and spirit, and sits croakingly asking,

"And must I thus forever live,
At this poor dying rate?"

as thousands are now doing upon the West Coast of Africa.

The struggle with the fever is not so much after all against death as against laziness—not so much for life as for energy. In my diary I find this entry, made in Africa: "I am beginning to feel lazy. Is this acclimating? I have a disposition to sit down! Alas! alas! my poor energy, is it falling a prey to this poisonous atmosphere?"

It would not profit the reader to have the symptoms of African fever described. I should not, however, omit from this chapter a few statements of a general therapeutical nature. Colonizers, merchants, political officials, teachers, and missionaries will go, in even greater numbers in the future than in the past, to meet and struggle with African fever. They should go to the West Coast, not only with the purpose of keeping their health, but also with a general idea of the course of treatment that they should pursue.

In the first place, it is absolutely necessary to keep the bowels open. The climate has a tendency to produce relaxation, and too much care can not be exercised. Tamar Indien, Eno's Fruit Salt, and castor oil are most excellent laxatives. For torpidity of the liver, which manifests itself in loss of appetite, a coated tongue, and heavy, yellowish eyes, the usual remedies are podophillyn powders or pills, or compound cathartic pills, taken overnight, and followed next morning by a seidlitz-powder, if necessary.

Certain symptoms precede fever. The person to be attacked loses his appetite; his skin gets dry, and he feels somewhat chilly. I look upon medicine as a necessary evil. It should be avoided as much as possible. Hence, my first effort to throw off African fever took the form of a brisk walk, or vigorous exercise with the axe. Sometimes this brings on perspiration and affords much relief. But if this natural course of treatment should fail, the patient should drink a hot tea of lemon or lime, or of the leaves of what is called "the fever bush"; then either get into bed, or, what is much better, wrap up in shawl or blanket, and throw himself on the sofa and "sweat it out."

This fever would be a simple ailment, were it not for the fact that malaria lingers in the system. It fastens itself upon the vitals and sticks closer than a brother. Hence quinine, in some form, is an indispensable remedy. Its effects, however, are often very injurious. It cures, but it also blights. It affects the hearing and the sight, and is harmful in many other respects. I used a medicine called Paschall's Fever and Ague Mixture,* which can not be too highly recommended. Quinine is undoubtedly an ingredient; but it is in such a proportion to other ingredients that one escapes the injurious effects experienced from taking quinine alone. It answers all the purposes of quinine pills, and, for the reason given, is infinitely better.

The fever leaves the patient in a feeble condition. Often the stomach and digestive organs fail to properly perform their work. I found that seltzer water, and such liquids as extract of beef, were very helpful to a debilitated stomach, and pepsin very stimulating to the digestive organs. *Spirituous liquors are positively injurious.* They have wrecked more lives on the coast than African fever; and they have been the devil's special agent in the destruction of character.

I have now set forth fairly and squarely my impressions of the climate of the West Coast. It is not healthy; yet it is not deadly. It is severely trying to the system of the foreigner; but the man of African blood, although not a native of the Coast, stands the climate better than either a Caucasian or a Mongolian. A Negro-American will thrive where the European can hardly live.

Europeans, who do business on the Coast, at the Gambia, Sierra Leone, Liberia, Lagos, Congo, contract to remain at their posts only from two to three years of continuous service. When they leave to recruit in their own *habitat*, their faces are yellow and bloodless, their eyes sunken and glassy, and their bodies thin and emaciated. One sees on the steamers bound from the West Coast to Europe a cadaverous-looking set of white men, who never fail to call

---

* Sold by Edward S. Morris, 4 South Merrick Street, Philadelphia.

forth hearty commiseration. Some of them have to be carried aboard the vessels on stretchers ; and they begin to recuperate as soon as they breathe the pure air of the sea for a few days.

If white men could thrive on the West Coast, they would flock to it as they have done to South Africa, and assert their "divine right to rule" the land and subjugate the aboriginal population to their proud sway, as the Caucasians invariably do wherever they are able to congregate in large numbers. Their arrogance and intolerance and pride, begotten of their leadership in the march of civilization, are seen in their unjust contact with China and their outrageous course in India. In North and South Africa they hold sway; but God reserves Tropical Africa for the Negro race. He has stationed climate there as a gloomy, watchful sentinel, with special orders against white men. Hence all their efforts of centuries to penetrate the country have resulted in disastrous failures; and throughout the lands they inhabit the cry has gone, "It is a deadly climate; the white man's grave."

I stopped, in 1884, at Freetown, Sierra Leone. The Queen's Advocate, a white man, was acting for both the Governor and the Chief-Justice, who were white men. I asked after them, and I was told that they had gone to the island of Madeira to recuperate. The climate was telling upon their systems. This is an illustration of what Mr. Spurgeon said about the deadly effect of the African climate upon the English Governors of Sierra Leone. They either die, or they retire to other climes, and thus get a new lease on life. On the return of the Governor and the Chief-Justice, the Queen's Advocate doubtless went off for his health.

I know that many who read these pages will differ from

my opinion, that a foreign Negro stands this trying African climate better than the Caucasian; but the thoughtful reader will readily see that there is more affinity in the blood of a pure Negro, although foreign born, for the African *habitat*, from which his ancestors came, than in a man who has had no connection direct or remote with Africa. Believing as I do, even without the gift of prophecy, I can see Ethiopia standing among the nations of the future, rejoicing in the triumphs of pure-blooded Ethiopians, who shall, in Tropical Africa, work out their great destiny, and prove equal to their illustrious ancestors, who "led the way, and acted as the pioneers of mankind in the various untrodden fields of art, literature, and science." *

CHAPTER IX.

RESOURCES—NATURAL AND CULTIVATED PRODUCTS—A GROWING COMMERCE.

STANLEY is criticised and denounced as an enthusiast and an optimist, because he gives such glowing accounts of the vast resources of the Congo; but he does not exaggerate in the least. The rapidly increasing African trade proves conclusively that there must be something in the Dark Continent after which to send the great ships of commerce from European and American ports.

Rich and varied are the resources of the Americo-African Republic. The soil contains gold, silver, and iron in great abundance. The iron ore is said to yield sixty per cent.; and it is found near the surface. The natives use

---

* Rawlinson's "Five Great Monarchies," Vol. I., p. 75.

gold and iron in certain crude manufactures; and they do not mine for these metals. English capitalists are digging gold at Axim, south of Liberia; and a superintendent of these mines, on his return to the coast from Scotland, told me that the same rich vein which he had struck at Axim certainly passes through Liberia. There can be no question about this. President Johnson, now in office, January, 1886, in denouncing a loan which a previous administration made in England, said, "I had heard whispers of a foreign loan. . . . . I besought you to go to the mines of Beulay and Medina, if you wanted gold, and not sell your country for British gold."* Capital, however, is needed to utilize these precious metals that lie in the bowels of the African Continent; and capital has been slow in finding its way to the West Coast, and especially to the Negro Republic.

The resources of the forests are inexhaustible; and they are within the reach of simple industry. Neither skilled labor nor capital is necessary to secure many of them. Palm-trees are found in great abundance, and they yield annually an enormous quantity of nuts and oil. Camwood and rubber-trees also abound, and are very valuable as articles of export. Millions of dollars go annually out of Europe and America to the West Coast; thousands go to Liberia, to purchase palm oil, palm nuts, camwood, and rubber. To these should be added ivory, which is one of the most valuable articles of trade, and which lies around in parts of the interior like common rocks.

But with these exceptions the forests of Liberia are untouched. They contain different varieties of valuable timber, suitable for almost any purpose. Growing almost everywhere are mahogany, oak, hickory, poplar, rose-

---

* Oration at Monrovia, July 26, '82.

wood, mulberry, and other valuable trees which could be secured easily and at little cost, for timber, furniture, and decorative work.

Then there is a great variety of fruit trees. Oranges, limes, guavas, plantains, pine-apples, plums, cocoanuts, bananas, pawpaws, rose-apples, sour sops, and others grow everywhere, and are remarkable for their delicious flavor. They may be seen in the streets, in the woods, on all sides. An independent fortune could be made by preserving and exporting these fruits. A captain running to the Liberian coast told me that he could easily sell all the guava preserves that the Republic could furnish.

I am sure I do not exaggerate when I say that the Americo-African Republic has within its territory, and lying back of it, regions of immense value that centuries of development could not exhaust. Commodore R. W. Shufeldt, a retired officer of the United States Navy, has had considerable experience in observation and exploration on the West Coast and in Liberia. In a letter to Dr. G. W. Samson under date of September 21, '85, he says: "In fact Liberia lies in front of the most fertile and most densely populated portions of the continent."

The soil of Liberia is very rich. It may be cultivated with a stick. If it is simply scratched and the seed dropped in, there is an abundant harvest.

Most of the vegetables may be raised, such as Guinea corn, sweet potatoes, beans, tomatoes, okra, watermelons, cabbages, and turnips. The natives cultivate a vegetable somewhat like the American sweet potato, which they call *eddoes*, and another like the turnip, which they call *cassavas*. I have seen all of these vegetables grown, and have cultivated many of them myself.

The Americo-Africans raise and export principally coffee and sugar. There is no reason why they should not add to these articles ginger, pepper, ground-nuts, indigo, arrowroot, and cotton. Everywhere, in a wild state, cotton is found; and it is of excellent fibre. Of course it is short, but cultivation would doubtless make it equal to the best staple in the world. Enterprise and industry, backed by a little capital, could accomplish great results where Nature is so lavish of her gifts of forests, soil, and field; for there is a limitless growth of plants, out of which the most valuable and useful medicines could be made.

The coffee of Liberia is the best in the world. It is indigenous; it grows wild everywhere. Hull, in his excellent book on Coffee Culture, gives the Liberian coffee the very first place. It is superior to Java or Mocha, both in the size of the berry and the deliciousness of the flavor. Ship-loads of scions have been exported to Brazil; and much of the superior American coffee is the product of the African scion. I have been told both in Europe and America that there could be created a special and wide demand for Liberian coffee, if it could be secured in such quantities as to justify efforts to create a market. Mr. C. T. Geyer, an enterprising New York merchant, who has visited the West Coast of Africa and the coffee farms of Liberia, writes me under date of December 16, 1885:

"I am pleased to make the following comments on Liberian coffee, having imported and dealt in it for many years. The berry is acknowledged by the trade to be the handsomest in the market; and it makes the strongest coffee. Those who have used it and acquired a taste for it will have no other. One great drawback to its increased use has been the limited quantity of it that has been raised. Within a few years coffee grown in the island of Ceylon from plants obtained in Liberia, has been upon the market as Liberian. I believe the best article of commerce Liberians can raise is coffee. It took the first medal at the Centennial Exhibition, in 1876; and it is universally regarded as the best coffee raised anywhere in the world."

Mr. Edward S. Morris, of Philadelphia, who lived for a time in Liberia; who has done much in promoting the culture of coffee there; and who, since 1856, has been selling it in the United States, is the inventor of a machine for hulling and cleaning the Liberian coffee. The berry is so large and hard that the mills used in other countries do not meet the requirements. Whenever foreign capital is turned toward the West Coast for investment, coffee culture will be one of the industries that will be safe and highly remunerative.

What a rich field for commercial enterprise the Americo-African Republic presents, with its vast resources of soil and woods, and the richest region of Africa lying back of it! The time certainly must come when the people of the United States will interest themselves in some special way in the growth and perpetuity of their first and only quasi colonial enterprise, and in the enlargement of its commerce. The mills of New England will send their manufactures, and the South and the West will send certain of their wares to Liberia, and bring back in their ships of commerce the gold, the ivory, and the coffee of this favored land.

Europeans are pushing their enterprises into the Americo-African Republic with all their might. The Germans, Dutch, and Belgians have stores, called "factories," at every port; and their business seems to be increasing yearly. English steamers stop at most of the Liberian ports to deliver cargo, and to take away the produce and natural treasures of the fields and forests. The French have just begun to send steamers to Liberian ports. Petition was made by the French to the National Legislature (1884) for rights and privileges in common with other foreigners; and it was readily and gladly granted. There are no American business houses on the Liberian coast, except a very small one at Cape Palmas; but three firms send their vessels to these "ports of entry," and trade from the harbors. They are great movable stores or "factories," floating on the water. They bring everything; the necessaries, the luxuries, and "the destructives"; food, raiment, delicacies, and wines, liquors, and segars. Yates & Porterfield, and Carlton & Moffat, of New York, and R. Lewis & Co., of Portland, Maine, send their vessels to the Liberian coast. The first-named firm has been doing for years a very large business, and are said to have grown wealthy out of the profits of the trade.

Every decade white men retire from the West Coast trade rich enough to live comfortably at home in Europe on their income. But they went into business on the coast with large capital behind them, usually representing companies with millions of dollars invested in ships, machinery, etc. The Liberian merchant plods on year after year, unable to enlarge his business because he does not have the capital. The foreigner adds thousands of dollars annually to his enterprises, puts his own vessel in the trade, and increases the number yearly; and as a natural result he grows independent in a few years, brings out a successor from Germany, England, France, or Holland, and retires to live at ease with "the dear ones all at home." But such is life. It is true, as Benjamin Franklin said, "To make money, one must have money."

Foreigners, finding that they "strike oil" in the Liberian trade, are quietly pushing to have their privileges enlarged. To them may be attributed the movement "to open the constitution," as it is called. They want two things granted them, for which they openly agitate. First, the right to lease land for a term of at least one hundred years; and, secondly, the right to establish trading posts up the rivers and in the interior, from which they are now excluded. The privileges of citizenship, and the right to vote and hold office, they are secretly working for.

The National Legislature (1884) opened three new ports of entry—San Pedro, Manna, and Niffou. Foreigners have the right to trade at them. Pushing and persistent as are the Europeans and white Americans, my impression is that their getting into the interior and up the rivers with their rum, tobacco, cloth, salt, and brass kettles, is only a question of time. It will certainly be the means of developing the interior trade of Liberia which is not yet touched. In the harbor of Freetown, Sierra Leone, one sees life, activity, bustle. I saw the harbor white with the sails of commerce—steamers, brigs, barks, schooners, sloops, native trading cutters, and row-boats, scores of them taken all together. Looking at them, I involuntarily exclaimed: "This is business!"

I may here presume that the reader asks a natural question: Are the Americo-Africans (the colored people of American birth or descent) profiting from the wealth of their country, and growing rich? Although I have not come to write about the people yet, I pause here to answer this pertinent inquiry with an emphatic *No!* The Americo-Africans would profit from the natural wealth of their country if they themselves had money to develop it, or could induce foreigners to invest their capital more largely than they do.

Emigrants from Europe to America, in its early history,

either brought money with them, or they had influence enough at home to draw capital after them. Even now American bonds and stocks are prominent on the English financial exchanges, and British capital has done much, and it is still doing a great deal, for the internal development of the United States—sustaining railroads, constructing bridges, conducting manufactories, and mining enterprises. A country may be ever so rich in its natural resources, but capital is required to make these resources available. What good would the gold discovered in California have done to business industries had not Eastern capital gone West, bored rocks, sunk shafts, erected machinery, dug up the precious metal, and then prepared it for circulation? There is money in a wholesale and retail tobacco house; but suppose some enterprising colored Americans should start this business, what would be the result? After we have built our establishment, stocked it, and secured our trading cutters, the white merchants and ship-owners who would bring us our tobacco, and who sell it themselves on the coast, would not consent to be driven out of the trade—no, not even to share it with us! They would run our freight up so high that our profits would be reduced to nothing. Indeed, it is probable that we should lose money by the venture! *But if this Negro Company could put their own ships upon the sea, then they would be masters of the situation!* This is the key to the solution of the business problem, so far as it concerns the Liberians or the American Negroes. We must have our own vessels upon the ocean carrying our African workers, our civilization, and our wares to the "Fatherland," and bringing back its riches.

Says a high commercial authority: "Outside of their colonies the principal advantages possessed by British and

French traders in Africa are their magnificent steamship lines, and their long-established resident agencies or branch houses."* I am glad to know that American Negroes are thinking in this direction. Making this reference to a New York audience in 1882, I was cheered to the echo; and addressing the Hampton Institute Alumni Association, in May, 1884, the same expression was most heartily applauded.

Our references have been mainly to Liberian merchants. We must bear in mind that Liberia is an exclusively Negro government. White men, therefore, are cautious as to making investments. Indeed, there is very little foreign capital in business in Liberia. Neither Europeans nor Americans seem to have sufficient confidence in the country to entrust their moneys to Liberians, and to invest it in business through them. It is different at Sierra Leone and Lagos, which are English possessions.

There are many Negroes who are wealthy merchants in both places. On my way to Liberia, there was on our steamer a Lagos merchant, a native African, returning from England with his family, a wife and two children. They were accompanied by a nurse and a valet. They had occupied apartments in London at "the West End," the aristocratic quarters. He had on board $50,000 worth of goods, and a small steam yacht for trade on the Niger. I was told that the trade of the West Coast is passing slowly into native African hands. But that is perfectly natural. Europeans can not stand this climate. It costs more to send and sustain one European in Western Africa than to do business through three African merchants. Business men are eminently practical; they do that which pays. The native merchant has the vantage ground; Africa is

---

* *The American Mail and Export Journal*, March, 1883, p. 115.

the Negro's country. His controlling it *in every respect* is only a question of time. The Romans held England; the Normans once ruled the country; but in the fulness of time God brought those to the front to whom He had given the land.

God, not we, "divided to the nations their inheritance," and "separated the sons of Adam." * The Negro has for his portion Central-Tropical Africa, and no other race will supplant, or permanently rule him on that soil. But in the fulness of God's time, kings and priests and merchants of Ethiopia shall influence, as they have already begun to do, the destinies of other countries and other races.

CHAPTER X.

PEOPLE—THE NATIVES—THEIR CUSTOMS AND MANNERS.

THE people of the Americo-African Republic are divided into two classes: (1). The Aborigines, who are, (*a*) the indigenous tribes, and (*b*) the slaves recaptured from slave-ships and returned to Africa; and (2). The colored colonizers from the United States and the West Indies, and their descendants.

The Natives, as the Aborigines are called, numbering about 800,000 persons, are divided into tribes, named Veys, Mandingoes, Kroos, Golahs, Greboes, Pessehs, Bassas, and Deys. They differ in dialect, as do the people of Great Britain even to-day. The Welsh, the Scotch, and the English are different and distinct dialects. The general appearance of the tribes is alike, except the

---

* Deut. xxxii. 8.

Mandingoes, who are a tall and sinewy race of men. One can always distinguish a Krooman. He is the sailor of the coast. He navigates all the steamers and ships that do business in West African waters. The Krooman was never a slave; he was too useful to the slave-trader as a sailor. In order to prevent the exportation of a Krooman, the tribe adopted as a sign a blue band down the forehead. Every male child is tattooed, and he grows up with that stamp upon his face, of which he never fails to be proud.

A NATIVE TOWN.

These tribes dwell in towns, each town having its chief or headman. The houses are neatly constructed of bamboo. Many of them are oblong. The Veys live in conical-shaped dwellings, with a porch in which they usually hang a hammock of their own manufacture. The houses are comparatively neat, and the African wife prides herself in keeping her home tidy and in order. The ground serves as the floor, but they frequently spread their home-made mats upon it. This is much better than the sleepy people of Madeira; whose floors are of stone, and are usually bare. Some of these African-made mats are very pretty. They combine different colors in making them. They cover the dining-room and sitting-room of many a well-to-do Americo-African, who buys them from the skillful, industrious natives. In building their houses they use no nails, but a rope and a cord of their own make, which are as strong and as durable as anything manufactured in Europe or America.

Most people have the idea that the Negro at home is an idle being who sits around and does nothing. They will hardly believe that they have their smiths who work in iron and gold, their weavers of cloth, and their looms, their dyers, carpenters, merchants, teachers, doctors, and farmers; and are engaged in many of the pursuits common to our more advanced civilized life. This is true of many of the Liberian tribes. Among some, if not all of them, the various industries of life are pursued, even if in a feeble way.

The food of the natives consists of rice, cassava, beef, mutton, game, fish, palm oil, and palm butter; and their drink is water and palm wine. Every native family looks out for something to eat. One of the difficulties in connection with hired labor arises from this fact. The native man will leave your work to make his rice farm, so as to be sure of the staff of life. A month before the rains, in March and April, he clears his land. At the first sign of the beginning of the rains he burns the brushwood and weeds. He plants after the first rain. The soil being extremely fertile, the seeds spring up in a few days. He then makes his wives and children watch the crop till it is gathered. And they have to be very attentive, or the rice-birds, which are always on the alert, would destroy it in a very short time. In four months the crop is gathered. The rice is cut down on the stalk. The stalks are put up in bundles; and these are taken home and put in the top of the houses. They keep dry, and are taken down, beaten, winnowed, boiled, and eaten as needed. It is a picturesque sight to pass, as I have often done, through a native town and see the busy housewife get the rice ready for cooking. One sees many mortars, and hears the music of the descending pestles and the sweet chatter or laughter of "the blameless Ethiopians."

The native wife is a very good housekeeper. In her dwelling the pans, kettles, and basins are hung around the room in order. When she puts dinner on the rudely constructed table, she never sits down, but in your presence tastes a little from every dish, as a sign that she has put nothing in it to hurt you. It is called, "Taking the witch off."

I saw the African at home for the first time at the Isles de Los; an island on the West Coast. I was struck with their intelligent countenances and matchless physical development. Looking from the deck of the steamer into a merchant row-boat, I saw the stalwart fellows gather around what appeared to be a wash-basin filled with rice and palm oil. The African boatmen stuck their hands in, filled them with rice, squeezed it into a ball, then in the twinkling of an eye they tossed it down their throats; and the food disappeared without chewing! I looked on with wide-open eyes. They gulped the entire dinner. They boil their rice very soft and the palm oil helps it to pass

3*

through the organs of digestion. Strange to say, dyspepsia is unknown among the natives. Of course they chew their meats. After eating they invariably wash their hands, mouth, and teeth.

It would require a volume to write about their customs. Some are good, many are bad, and some are ludicrous. Their diversions would entertain and amuse. I attended a play by natives on Vey Island. Its effect was like that of a comic tragedy—ridiculous and grand, laughable and exciting! Instead of paying money to see the performance, I gave them tobacco; others gave cloth, beads, and caps. One thing appears to be true—"When the sun goes down, all Africa dances."

Two customs are interwoven with the warp and woof of their social system. They are evils which can not be removed except by slow moral processes. We refer to polygamy and slavery. The former evil, however, is not as wide-spread as one would suppose. Passing through Krootown one day, and seeing a Krooman building a house, I asked him how many wives he had. "Me no fit to have but two. Woman he be cost too much money," was the reply. And thereby hangs a tale. The African woman spends her money, or rather her husband's, just as an American or European wife does. An African lady sees her neighbor wearing a new pair of "anklets," or necklace, or bracelets. She must have a new set too; and she taunts her husband with his poverty if he does not respond to her appeals. Well, the African husband finds it uncomfortable to have a half dozen women begging or taunting him at the same time. Indeed, monogamists sometimes find it hard to keep up with the fancies and wants of "the lady of the house." It must also be remembered that an African wife costs money before she is secured. The man who wants a girl to wife must first get together the purchase-money in the form of oxen, bullocks, or some other article of trade. A woman has no choice in the matter of marriage. Often she is chosen while quite a child. A Krooman by the name of "Poor Fellow" took me, while I was passing through Krootown, to the dwelling of his affianced. He was a grown man; she was a little twelve-year-old girl. Poor Fellow was saving money to pay for her. She had already been promised him. The article was not to be delivered, however, till full payment was made.

The wife is property. She is in absolute submission to her husband. She never sits down to meals with him, and always treats him as her lord.

As in Holland and other parts of Europe, notably in the Alps, where wives are often seen hitched up with asses and plowing in the fields while their husbands guide the plow;* as in all barbarous countries, so also in Liberia among the natives, the women perform much physical labor. I have seen women in "the land of the Dutch" load and unload vessels, run the freight canal boats, and carry immense burdens. The African wife takes her axe, goes to the woods, and comes home with a huge pile of sticks on her head. It is perfectly wonderful to see the loads women carry on the head; and they can keep them there, and even dance, without touching them with their hands.

The African wife is not an idle, useless being. She washes the clothes, looks after the house, and cooks. She boils rice to perfectiom. She rises with the sun, goes to the spring for water, takes up the mats from the stationary beds, which are used during the day as settees, brushes up, arranges things in order, then cooks the break-

---

* Foster's Cyclopedia, p. 668.

fast. I have seen her varied daily experiences morning, noon, and afternoon. I have seen her going to and returning from the spring, busy in her dwelling, cooking outside, looking after the children, bathing them, and oiling and braiding their hair.

The traveller is familiar with the dress of the native African. He wears a girdle about his loins, and a wide piece of cloth, manufactured by his wife, thrown loosely across his left shoulder and wrapped around his body. It is like the kilt worn by the Scottish Highlander. The Mandingoes wear a long, loose flowing robe, usually made out of white cloth of their own manufacture.

I think, of course, that the African can improve on both the quantity and style of his dress. I except the Mandingoes. But I do not believe that they will ever adopt European or American garments and style. They ought not to do so. They are not suited to their climate. Dressed as they are, these Liberian natives could appear in Hyde Park or on Broadway without violating the decencies of life. Of course, they would create an excitement; but so does the East Indiaman in London, and the Chinaman in New York. After all it is a question of comfort, custom, and taste.

Some of the women are very handsome. One can see nowhere in the world better specimens of natural beauty. They carry themselves like queens. The Vey women are especially handsome. Their expression and form are charming. Their feet are perfectly symmetrical and delicately small. Their eyes and teeth would be envied by a Parisian belle. "Thou art black and comely," could be applied to a Vey woman without hesitation.

The native women wear a piece of cloth which extends from their waist down to their ankles. The cloth is sometimes a prettily-dyed specimen of their own skillful making; but near the coast one often sees imported cloth worn with pride by those who can afford it. African women, like American women, prefer foreign goods. It sounds "bigger" than "home-made." Around their necks, ankles, and wrists they wear flashy ornaments. It is amusing to see the variegated adornments of an African lady. We smile just as we would at a Dutch peasant, or at the Apostle of Æstheticism. The hair is always done up with scrupulous care. These women have "fleecy locks"; but they do their hair up so as to charm "the civilized man." It is something wonderful. When they get through combing, plaiting, braiding, and adorning, they look exceedingly well.

Such is the picture of an African woman. A head done up with neatness, skill, and taste; a piece of cloth extending from the waist to the ankles; gold or some other kind of adornments around neck, wrists, and ankles. There she stands; and you involuntarily repeat what the queen of Sheba may have inspired Solomon to say, "Thou art black and comely."

A part of her body is exposed, it is true; but nobody has evil thoughts or evil desires. The stranger, visiting Edinburgh, Scotland, turns and looks long and admiringly at the beautifully shaped limbs of the fish-wives of Newhaven, whose dresses are as short as those of school-girls. The stranger may have evil thoughts; but the Scotchman never thinks about those charming women who go about their streets with exposed limbs selling fish to whoever may buy. It is so in Liberia with the native women. No one notices a woman's bust, or arms, or limbs other than to think of specimens of painting and sculpture, and go on his way saying to himself, "Art may imitate, but it can not equal nature."

The natives living in the territory of Liberia have rules and laws of their own; but they acknowledge, to some extent, the general oversight and control of the Republic. Their governments are monarchical, as a rule. Their kings, chiefs, or headmen inherit their position and authority. Native kings have attended the Liberian Legislature and participated in its deliberations. Two native delegates from the Grebos sat in the last House (1884). The intention is to give the native element even larger representation in the future than in the past, going as far as practicable in the matter. Of course, to grant general representation, that is, in proportion to numbers, would be to subjugate the Americo-Liberian civilization to native Paganism and Mohammedanism.

Men write about "the savages of Africa." The geographies read, "Central Africa is an unexplored region, inhabited by savage tribes of Negroes." There can be no question as to the existence of savages. There are some tribes which have been made savages by the infamous slave-trade conducted for centuries by Europeans and white Americans; but, as a rule, the natives of Central-Tropical Africa are kind, hospitable, good-natured, trustful to a fault. Their confidence can be more easily secured than any people on the face of the earth, because their natural *bonhomie* leads them to trust; and they too easily forgive and forget wrongs, because of the natural buoyancy of their character. Mungo Park is sick unto death among them. They nurse him till he gets well, and send him away with this parting blessing:

> "Go, white man, go; but with thee bear
> The Negro's wish, the Negro's prayer;
> Remembrance of the Negro's care."

Livingstone dies in the interior of Central Africa, and

willing Negro hands bear him over hills and through valleys and jungles and swamps, until they deliver his lifeless body to the white men, who dwell by the shores of the far-resounding Indian Ocean.

If in interior Africa, if on the coast, if in the North or in the South, they have shot into and destroyed exploring expeditions, it has been because white men, in order to get slaves, have burnt down their towns and carried into bondage their women and their children, and produced such impressions as made them savage and revengeful. Even explorers, when opposed, have fought their way through a country in which they had no rights except such as were granted them. Africa, for centuries, has been robbed and mobbed; and yet, man's inhumanity to man has only made her countless millions mourn.

I have heard of African honesty and hospitality from the lips of white and black travellers, men unknown to literature or fame, and yet who as merchants, missionaries, and explorers have seen much of the interior. Being strangers, they were given "the best house" and "the very best fare." Being at the mercy of the natives, they slept with their purse exposed to view, and yet never lost a dollar. One man lost a package fully fifty miles from town. On his arrival, he reported his loss to the king. On rising next morning, the package was handed him, having been found by natives passing over the same road. Read the criminal records of Christendom, and then hear our challenge to find more good-heartedness, more honesty anywhere than we find among the natives of Africa, especially those who are removed from the evil influences of the coast.

But some people will not believe in the honesty of the natives. I gave some stubborn facts to a white man on one occasion. His reply was, "Well, that may be true: but it is to be ascribed not to innate honesty, but to their fear resulting from superstition." I deny it. England once was as Liberia is. I speak of the natives. As a French writer says, " M. Guizot tells us that Alfred, to put the honesty of his subjects to the test, used to cause bracelets of gold to be hung up in public places. They were never stolen ; and if a traveller dropped his purse by the roadside, he had no need to turn back and seek it, for he was certain to find it untouched, even though he did not pass that way again for a month. Such was the Saxon in the time of Alfred the Great."

Such are many of the African tribes to-day. But European commercial intercourse is certainly somewhat demoralizing. First, the slave-trade came like a dragon to bite, to poison, to kill. And now Christian nations are continuing their damnable work by sending rum to "the heathen in Africa." True, they send missionaries. But they first make Africa sick, then they send in the doctor; they give poison, then they administer an antidote. So did Spain deal with Africa when she sent her priests in her slave-ships. So does Great Britain treat "the Dark Continent" to-day in sending her missionaries in her rum-ships. No wonder that Catholic cathedrals and monasteries are decaying in the Congo valley! No wonder that the natives turned from the priest and the crucifix in disgust! No wonder that Protestant Christianity has an up-hill work! No wonder that the tipsy African recently said, in reply to the rebuke of the European missionary : " Be he no your brudder who send us rum? Go talkee him ; no talkee me!"

CHAPTER XI.

PEOPLE—THE KROO AND THE VEY TRIBES.

THESE two tribes are especially useful and distinguished. Both the Kroos and the Veys have towns near Monrovia, the capital of Liberia. I saw more of them than of any of the other tribes.

The Kroomen are the first people one meets on the West Coast. They are the sailors. They are in the sea from infancy. I have seen little girls and boys that could hardly walk, playing in the water as the child of an interior town would play in the sand. At Sierra Leone or Monrovia, Kroo sailors board every vessel bound down the coast. It is an interesting change from white sailors to black sailors, and from a known to an unknown tongue. White sailors, hardy though they be, are not equal to the task of taking a vessel from Sierra Leone to the Congo, and bringing her back. The sun, the rain, the night air, and the dew would enfeeble them in a fortnight. They would sicken and die before they reached the Cameroons. These Kroomen are indispensable. They were found to be so in the days of the slave-trade, hence every Krooman is able to make the proud boast: "I have never been a slave."

Being sailors, the Kroomen are of a roving disposition. Their highest ambition is to cross the deep blue sea. Many of them have been "abroad"; and they become "lions" on their return. The "lions" delight to gather their less fortunate brethren around them and expatiate on the wonders of "the white man's country."

It is amusing to see some of them on their return from "abroad." Of course they must dress "white man fash";

and they parade themselves to the amusement of the European and American, and to the envy of many of their fellow-comrades. I have seen a returned Krooman wearing a Prince Albert diagonal coat buttoned up to his neck, but not another article of clothing did he have on—no shoes, pants, shirt, collar, or hat—nothing but his "girdle about his loins" and his "Prince Albert"! But he strutted around "Allee same like 'Merican man"! I have seen a Krooman in English walking-coat, silk hat, and umbrella, but no shoes! Many amusing pictures could be drawn.

These Kroomen return home with singular names. The sailors must palm them off on their confiding Ethiopian comrades as "proper 'Merican," or "'ristocratic English." One day, at Krootown, I asked a lad who had been with his father on an English man-of-war, and who could speak a little English: "Bubbs, what is your name?" "Little Potato," was the reply. "What is your father's name?" I laughed aloud on receiving for answer, "Big Potato." They take a pride in such names as "Two Pound Ten," "Pea Soup," "Jumping Jack," "Poor Fellow," etc. Two brothers returned from a man-of-war. I asked one of them on Kroo beach: "What is your name?" "Jack Savage," he answered. "What is your brother's name?" "John Savage." The steward on board of a West Coast vessel, on which I was a passenger, told me that his name was Dick Richard, and it was a long time before I could make any change in such a peculiar cognomen. We changed several names. "Little Potato" is now known as "Toussaint L'Ouverture," and "Poor Fellow" is called "Hannibal." After all, "what's in a name?" But it is barbarous to make a man, who knows no English, call himself "Slow Coach."

These Kroomen have no respect for titles. They are

very democratic; they are perfectly courteous and respectful when they call you by your surname, without any prefix whatever. I was surprised beyond expression to hear the United States Minister's hired Kroo head-boatman say, "Smit, are you going boat-riding to-day?" For six weeks the Kroo steward on board our homeward-bound vessel occasionally amused me by asking, "Stewart, can I do anything for you?" I never corrected him till the end of the voyage, when I gave him a few points on American etiquette.

My impression is that the Krooman is a very mercenary fellow. His contact with white men in trade has made him so, however. He will beg if he is dying, and charge you for telling his name; but he is a manly fellow, and if he gets attached to you, there is nothing that he will not do for you.

The Kroos are neat and cleanly; the women bathe three times a day. They use a wonderful amount of water. One of the most picturesque sights I have ever seen in my life was the Krootown girls and women going to and coming from the spring, in the early morning and the late afternoon, with tubs, buckets, and barrels of water balanced on their heads, while they laughed, talked, sang, and danced.

A Krooman thinks there is no place like home, and no person in the world like mother. The attachment of grown men to their mothers is childlike and truly touching. This is natural. Polygamy gives a man several families and homes; but the children have only one hut and one mamma. Father is often away—never in one house long; but mother is always present to decide the little disputes, to satisfy the little stomachs, to sing away the little pains and sorrows. The sweetest name on Krooman tongue is "mother."

Seeing New York for the first time from the deck of a vessel, a Krooman went into ecstasies. He was asked if he would not like to live in that great city. "No," was the quick reply. "Why?" asked the astounded American. The answer was readily given, "No Krooman live here; no Kroowoman. No Kroo own house." The reason given me by a Kroo steward for not living in New York was, "Can't leave mammy." He was fully thirty-five years of age. Enterprising and progressive, the Kroos, under the stimulus of a righteous commerce and a truly Christian civilization, will become a powerful force in African regeneration.

The Veys are the tribe which take the first place in Liberia. They are barbarians or "heathen" *magis natione quam ratione*. In what makes manly character, in what makes intellectual strength, the Veys rank with any people. They have invented their own alphabet, constructed their own written as well as spoken language, and they are slowly growing a literature. They use a pen and an indelible ink that they make themselves. I have often visited Veytown and looked with pride upon these representatives of the Ethiopian race, who show that they possess the highest order of intellect. I admire the Mandingoes, because they are learned in the Koran and the Commentaries; but their books are borrowed from the Arabic. I go into inexpressible enthusiasm over the Veys; because they are not only versed in Arabic lore, but because, as has already been said, they also have their own language in which they speak and write; and they have a growing literature. May they be speedily brought in contact with a better civilization, and receive the benefits of a truly Christian education.

It is a mistake to suppose these Liberian natives simple, ignorant creatures. My impression is that they are naturally superior to the average Negro who has been crushed by the monster, slavery. They are keen, bright, quick-witted, able to distinguish the genuine from the sham. Let the reader remember that the Veyman lives in his neatly constructed dwelling; that he has his own written language, and is acquainted with Arabic literature, and can converse in that Asiatic tongue as well as in the English! Is that man to be despised? No; I have often felt his comparative superiority! Since seeing them, I do not wonder at the brains found among Negroes in the land of their captivity. Theodore Dwight, Esq., says that between 1770–5, a report reached England that a young African slave in Maryland could read and write Arabic, and was well versed in Arabic literature. His name was Job-ben-Solomon. He was released, sent to England, and there assisted Sir Hans Sloane, the able scholar and founder of the British Museum, in translating several Arabic works.* Much has been done in Liberia to promote Christian civilization and education among the natives. They respond everywhere to outside influences, Africanizing them, and using them to develop their country and to promote its welfare. May the good work go on until Ethiopia shall rise from her reclining position and stand upon her feet to illustrate the poet's prophecy:

"Time's noblest offspring is the last."

---

* *Methodist Quarterly Review*, January, 1869.

CHAPTER XII.
PEOPLE—THE AMERICO-AFRICANS.

THE emigrants from the United States and the West Indies and their descendants are called "Liberians." They were sent out by the American Colonization Society. Up to January 1, 1867, 13,136 emigrants had gone to Liberia, and the United States Government had returned to Africa 5,722 recaptured slaves. But since 1867 there has been a remarkable decrease in the number of colored people who have left America for Africa. The Colonization Society pays the emigrant's passage and provides for his maintenance for six months.

We must candidly say that the Americo-Africans in Liberia are not in such a condition as to call forth our enthusiasm. We refer to the masses, not to the few. Most of the colored people who have emigrated to Africa were poor and comparatively ignorant. In this new country and hostile climate, they have enjoyed neither the support of large capital nor the direction of general intelligence. They carried to Africa very little idea of voluntary, systematic labor. They worked in America more from outside than inside influences. Finding themselves free to lie down and to rise up, and having been supported by the Colonization Society, they have done very little work. I have seen Liberians who went to the West Coast, with reputations for industry, sitting idly in dilapidated or rudely constructed houses, or walking around abusing the Government for not opening roads and building bridges, thus creating prosperity; or these demoralized individuals would exhaust their vocabulary in abusing their neighbors, characterizing them as the meanest and most devilish of mankind. Then some have plainly said, "I worked hard enough when I was a slave. Here I can lie down when I want to and get up when I please; and there is no one to molest or make me afraid."

The motto of the Republic is, "The love of liberty brought us here." Many Liberians make this to mean, "To be free from labor we came here." True to their old Southern training, a large class of the people look upon labor as degrading, as fit only for menials. This spirit, however, is not as wide-spread as in former years. Wages are low. Fifteen dollars can buy a native boy "apprentice" for a term of years. Twenty-five cents a day and meals are considered fair. Four dollars a month is average wages even for Liberian help. But it costs in one way and another to have a retinue of servants. They must be fed, clothed, and housed. This is a luxury only for those upon whom Fortune has smiled. But as the Liberians are eminently democratic, the poor imitate the rich and render themselves both pitiable and ludicrous. I have seen many amusing pictures in Monrovia.

I have seen a barefooted little girl about ten years of age, dressed in poor calico, on her way to school, and a native boy about twelve, half naked, carrying her primer! I have seen a boy on the back of a native lad, using the unfortunate son of the soil in place of a Shetland pony! There are no ponies, no donkeys, no little carts to ride to school in; so native boys are often substituted. It is not in keeping with the dignity of a gentleman or lady to carry a bundle in the streets. Such is the general sentiment. There are honorable and pronounced exceptions; but, as a general rule, the Americo-Africans have carried with them old Southern ideas of labor. An eminent gentleman, having been called to a high and responsible position in the Republic to which he must devote all his time and energy, had to give up his coffee-farm. He advertised for some one to take charge of it. He told me that it was amusing to hear the applicants tell how much work they could make a native man do. They considered *that* their very best recommendation. But this gentleman, who is a man of great energy and thrift, would interrupt and astonish each applicant with the question, "How much work can *you* do?"

An orator, Abraham Smith, formerly of Mt. Pleasant, S. C., making an address in Planters' Hall, on the St. Paul's River, and rebuking his fellow-citizens for their false notions about labor, and denouncing many of their silly practices, brought his speech to a climax with the startling declaration, "YOU FREE TILL YOU FOOL." His remark created a sensation. The Liberian certainly gives a broad definition to freedom. He is, perhaps, the best living specimen of the democrat. He recognizes no social grades. Each man is a king. An American on visiting the President was surprised to hear him say to his butler, "*Mr. Ross*, please bring in the wine." This was six years ago.

Is it not to be wondered at that so little has been done in Liberia? The climate is against the people. Their education has been against them, and they have increased their weakness by lying down on native muscle, and depending too much on foreign philanthropy. Charity enfeebles the energies, destroys enterprise, and prevents self-reliance. No wonder that even after sixty years of opportunity, and thirty-seven years of national existence, there are no railroads, no manufactories, no steam or water-mills, no bridges, no horses or oxen in use, except at Cape Palmas! Practically little beyond what nature provides! I send for a barber to trim my hair. There is no barber-shop in Monrovia, a town of at least two thousand inhabitants, the capital and metropolis of the Republic. He comes. Ten years ago he was doing well in Augusta, Georgia. He brings neither cloth, towels, comb, brush, whisk-broom—nothing but an old pair of very dull scissors. I ask him, "How is this?" "Well," he replies, "I have stopped *barbarizing*." I talked to him about railroads and other enterprises. He complained of the poverty of the country and the slowness of the people, and said he had stopped thinking about such things, and then voiced the sentiment,

> "Man wants but little here below,
> Nor wants that little long."

The masses of colored people who have settled in Liberia went there with a wrong impression. They emigrated with the feeling that they were going to "a land flowing with milk and honey"; then when they found that to build up a Christian Negro Nationality, to establish a new and comfortable home for the family, and to bear the burdens of a great social, religious, and political experiment, required sacrifice, labor, pluck, and steadfastness, they were surprised, and became disappointed, discouraged, and despondent.

But this is not to be wondered at. Throw a man upon the West Coast comparatively penniless and with no regular habits of industry; put him to acclimate in some broken-down old house into which the water runs when it rains, and through which the Harmattan blows as through a sieve; give him poor food to eat for six months, and you make him an easy prey to death or "constitutional tiredness."

I have no sympathy, however, with disappointed persons who return to the United States and abuse Liberia.

The difficulties to be met there were largely encountered here by the early settlers. If the emigrant goes back from the coast, he can settle in a hilly country and enjoy health; but the Christian Negro is cursed by poverty. He can not carry capital to Liberia; and thereby hangs a tale. It is not the country. Money to put boats on the river, to build railroads, to drain the swamps, and to open up highways to the interior—this is what is needed. Capital in the hands of a population founded on aboriginal stock, and enjoying the benefits of Christian education, will solve the problem of life in Liberia. If I could influence the Colonization Society, I would earnestly plead with them to stop making emigration their objective point and use their funds mainly in internal improvements, opening roads, building bridges, fostering industries, and especially in establishing a system of agricultural and industrial education, beginning with the common schools.

A person who thinks of emigrating to Liberia should examine himself thoroughly as to his physical condition; more carefully than a volunteer is examined before he is permitted to enlist for the war. One needs all the vigor of mind and body that it is possible to command. The African fever invariably attacks and besieges the weakest part of our system. It develops the germ of any disease that may be in us; and, while running riot through our bodies, it makes us home-sick, fills us with home-longings; it makes us hanker after "the flesh-pots of Egypt," as a distinguished Liberian puts it. If the person meditating emigration be young, of strong constitution, and good health; and if he can live somewhat independent of the provisions of the Colonization Society, the chances of acclimating successfully are in his favor. If he can not meet these conditions, let him look well lest he leap into the dark; lest the battle of life be too severe for him.

Industry, strongly backed by health and a little capital, can reach competence and acquire wealth. More is not accomplished because these conditions do not abound. A man need not go to Liberia without money and expect to become independent easily or quickly. It is hard to get money; there is such a little in circulation. Those who have "cash" generally hold it. The circulating medium of trade may be said to be cloth, tobacco, and salt food. Domestic debts are paid in "trade." I have heard laboring people testify, again and again, on this point. Even the small farmers find it hard, almost impossible, to sell their coffee for reasonable "cash" prices. The merchants prefer to deal in "trade." It is to their advantage to do so. I work for a man. He gives me an order on the store where he deals, and I go there and take my pay in trade. This makes it hard for a poor man to get hold of money. This condition of things stifles enterprise, especially in the cultivation of the soil. If an emigrant brings with him some cloth, tobacco, and a little cash; if he keeps his health, and is economical and judicious, he can plant coffee and in three years begin to gather a crop. He can cultivate sugar, which he may harvest annually. The coffee-tree does not commence to yield until from three to four years after the plant is set out. But when it does begin to bear, it yields continuously for about thirty years. The farmer sets out the scions, and then for the next thirty years he has simply to keep down the weeds and grass, stir the earth around the roots, and keep his farm clean. His annual harvest is sure. It is to be said, however, that one man, unaided, can not cultivate more than five acres of coffee; and the net profit per acre is not more than forty or fifty dollars, and I give the very highest estimate. It is hardly ever reached, I think. The man who can cultivate from fifty to one hundred acres is the farmer who counts his income by the thousands. The poor farmer, however, can increase his acreage every year. But climate and other conditions will make it a long time before a man, unaided by either capital or labor, can grow enough coffee to secure a comfortable income. The same may be said of sugar, with this difference: it is easier to cultivate coffee than sugar. The poor man can not own a sugar-mill; but he can sell his coffee right from the tree, in the hull.

The Government gives every married emigrant twenty-five acres of land, and every single man ten acres. Of course, it is covered with trees and a thick undergrowth. The emigrant must clear it and prepare it for planting; he then must buy coffee scions and set them out, and wait three years, perhaps four, for his crop. It is hard and trying work. There are no horses or oxen in use. He does not own stock himself, nor do his neighbors; he must walk to reach town or the nearest settlement; he must build his house; he must struggle hard if he would enjoy life. But after ten, twenty, aye, thirty years of earnest, faithful effort, he settles down under his own vine and fig-tree, a happy, contented, and wealthy farmer. I met a few of these in Liberia.

But while such are the possibilities, the present condition of the Americo-African is weak. The population needs energy; and it will take a mighty force to energize the whole Republic. Liberia needs a greater population representing the Christian civilization. She needs men; she needs capitalists; she needs teachers; she needs a supply, not of muscle, but of educated brains; money for business investments; people of force of character and push, who will make the wilderness to bloom, the rivers and bays to be white with the evidences of commercial activity, and the nation to shake off its stagnation and stand erect in the strength of general prosperity.

CHAPTER XIII.

PEOPLE—RELATION OF LIBERIANS AND NATIVES.

UNTIL within the past ten years, the relation between the native and the Negro emigrant from America has been that of master and slave. The former American slave treated the African freeman as if he had no rights which were worthy of respect! And that spirit has not altogether departed, although I am glad to say it is disappearing. This fact of the ill-treatment of the natives by the emigrants is not so strange after all; for the oppressed, when given an opportunity, generally become oppressors. The natives of Liberia have been to the emigrants from America just what these ex-slaves were to the whites of the South. They have been defrauded, beaten with stripes, and made to feel that they were inferior beings. They were excluded from the churches and the schools; given back-seats at the camp-meetings, if there were any to spare; and as to entering an emigrant's parlor or even front door, why, a native would never dream of it. While much of this snobbish spirit has departed, and while it is still decreasing, yet enough of it remains to make a decided impression upon the student of Liberian history and condition. I have seen a civilized native boy, who had studied a few months in England, frequently enter a house on a business errand by the back way; and the mistress of the house, a woman who cooked and washed in the United States for a living, wanted it to be distinctly understood, that her "front do'" was not to be used by "country people," as the natives are sometimes called.

One Sabbath morning several natives came into a church in Liberia. They were shown into back pews; they did not crowd them; they hardly filled them. But a thin-skinned female emigrant flounced out of the pew and out of the door with the air that an ill-bred white American woman would exhibit on changing her seat in a street-car because she was too near a "nigger." I thought that she had left not to return; but no; in a few moments she came back with a chair, which she placed far from the natives, in one of the aisles, and occupied it.

When the natives were not maltreated, they were made the objects of a scornful and contemptuous indifference. A native king, with his suite, was presented to one of the early Presidents of Liberia. His Excellency did not condescend to rise on receiving His Majesty. The king felt the insult; said nothing there and then, however, but he never returned or affiliated with the Liberians.

I am compelled to write the truth. Some facts I record with regret. It gives me, therefore, special pleasure to say that there are emigrants who have acted in a spirit of Christian charity, fairness, and liberality toward the natives. They have educated and Christianized native youth, and sent them back among their kinsfolk and acquaintances. I have discovered that, in many instances, there are ties of affection and friendship between the natives and the Americo-Africans that are as strong as if they were founded in blood-relationships.

In December, 1866, President Warner said to the National Legislature in his annual message: "But these chiefs and their subjects have, undoubtedly, certain rights,

A NATIVE PALAVER.

both natural and political, which should be highly respected by this Government and people. And when this is done, and *the natives are not provoked by us to the commission of lawless deeds*,* or instigated by dishonorable foreigners to insubordination, there will subsist between us and them a permanent good understanding and the greatest cordiality of feeling." This voice is being heeded now.

Since the last war with the natives, the Greboes of Cape Palmas in 1875, a radical change has taken place. The masses have not yet come to regard the native as "a man and a brother"; but the leaders of thought and public opinion are moving in the right direction, and a thorough revolution of the sentiment of the country is only a question of time. The native question is now prominent in every State paper, in legislation, in public addresses, and sermons; and at public dinners the education and civilization of the natives occupy a conspicuous place on the list of toasts that are proposed and replied to. There was a time when they were not admitted to the privileges of the college, or the schools, with Americo-Liberian children! Now the policy of school and college is to educate natives side by side with the Liberian youth.

Another one of the most hopeful features of the problem of life in Liberia is the fact that men of intelligence are marrying civilized native women. A former Secretary of State, an able lawyer, and a man of the broadest views, is married to a civilized Grebo lady; and she is a model wife and an excellent housekeeper, reserved yet intelligent, dignified yet cordial. This example, set in the highest circle and walk of life, is being followed by many intelligent and far-seeing young men. Intermarriages are common at Cape Palmas. I made my last visit to the Muhlenberg Mission,

---

* The *italics* are the author's.

conducted so ably and successfully by the Rev. D. A. Day, in January, 1884. Mr. Day told me that one of the leading young men of Arthington had written him asking permission to court a native girl then in the mission school. Arthington leads Liberia. Energy, thrift, industry, progress, and advanced views as to life in general and to the native question in particular, are better illustrated there than anywhere else in the Republic. The Liberian boy works in the coffee-fields, in the barn, and at the coffee-hulling mill side by side with the native youth. There is no difference. I visit the settlement. My satchel and bag are to be brought from the mission, two miles away. The most prominent citizen sends his son and a native boy there. What an example, teaching both boys the dignity of labor! No wonder that Arthington is the very embodiment of enterprise. Its history shows what can be done in Liberia with proper pioneers and a little capital. And yet even here the emigrants from America find it necessary to fight the hostile climate. Intermarriage with the natives will do much toward solving the difficult problem of Liberia's advancement. The Republic should not look mainly to America for its population. It should use its indigenous material in developing its great resources. What a difference between Sierra Leone and Liberia, between Freetown and Monrovia! In the English colony there are enterprise and push. I account for its superior advancement in two ways: first, the population is founded on an indigenous stock; and, secondly, capital has been judiciously employed in developing the people and the country. There must be a fusion between the Liberian and the native, a baptism of the spirit of labor, and the judicious introduction of Christian education and invested capital, if the Republic is to prosper.

4*

President Johnson says: "We have a population numerous, hardy, and industrious, devoted to agriculture and manufactures, when not seduced by the demon of war. I mean our aboriginal brothers. Where are we to get such muscle, such bone and sinew, to practice the arts of peace, and for defensive war? Where such intellects? Where such shrewdness in trade? And yet we are neglecting them. Had we discharged our duty to them, to-day the fruitful fields would be smiling with golden harvests all over the land; our seas would be whitened with the sails of commerce. . . . . Even in the science of government they excel us. . . . . In spite of our neglect of them, these chiefs and these tribes feel that they are one with us, and prefer living under the Liberian Government to being ruled by a foreign Government and an alien race." *

If I had to give a watchword to Liberia, it would be, "CHRISTIAN EDUCATION, INDUSTRIAL WORK, AND FUSION WITH THE NATIVES." Herein lies the salvation of the Republic. Go to almost any town or settlement in the country, and one sees the ruins of former buildings, farms, and stores. On every hand is apparent degeneracy and decay. The people revel in reminiscences of departed activity and prosperity. Why is this? Poverty and lack of push keep them on the coast, in the swamps, where malaria is king, sapping the energy, destroying the vitality, and rendering them spiritless. My impression is, that the Americo-Liberian is not productive in the third generation. This impression may not be correct; but I have noticed that the grandchildren of Americo-Liberians do not have children. Indeed, often the offspring of parents, who themselves were born and brought up in Liberia, are not healthy and hardy, but are puny and sickly. Let me

---

* An oration delivered in Monrovia, July 26, 1882.

put it this way: An American emigrant family marrying among fellow-emigrants, would become extinct after the third generation. My impression is that this would be true of any family in any part of the earth, making an absolute change of climate and physical environments, especially where the climate is unhealthy and the surroundings unfavorable. It is not to be wondered at, then, that the Liberian children bred, born, and reared in this malarial atmosphere grow weaker in both mind and body, as they get further removed from the parent stock. Let Christian education, work, and *fusion with the natives* be the watchword; and if Liberia be re-enforced by American Negroes of force of character, push, education, and earnestness, and if capital start with them and is economically used and judiciously invested, the Republic will enter upon an era of solid and permanent prosperity, and will become the pride of Negroes everywhere, and helpful to the civilization of Africa.

CHAPTER XIV.

PEOPLE—GENERAL CONDITION AND PROSPECTS.

UNTIL 1848 Liberia was a colony. Its machinery was under the control of the American Colonization Society of the United States.

But certain inconveniences and embarrassments were experienced. Because it was neither an independent nation nor an actual colony of the United States, Liberia suffered in her contact with the Powers of Europe; and the colonists themselves grew restless under laws made for them in the United States, and administered by an agent in whose appointment they had no voice.

The Society decided to give the colonists the right of self-government. In July, 1847, a convention of the people assembled in Monrovia, framed a Declaration of Independence and a Constitution which were adopted by the people at large July 26, 1847.

It is interesting to note the reasons given by the colonists in their Declaration of Independence for desiring to set up for themselves.

It opens with a reference to the fact that man has an inalienable right to life, liberty, and the pursuit of happiness. Among the reasons which are given for leaving the United States are these: (1) "In some parts of that country we are debarred by law from all the rights and privileges of men; in other parts public sentiment, more powerful than law, frowned us down"; (2). "We were everywhere shut out from all civil office"; (3). "We were excluded from all participation in the government"; (4). "We were taxed without our consent"; (5). "We were compelled to contribute to the resources of a country which gave us no protection"; (6). "We were made a separate and distinct class, and against us every avenue to improvement was effectually closed." The history of colonization is then succinctly stated. The fact is announced that "Questions have arisen which it is supposed can be adjusted only by agreement between sovereign Powers." Liberia is therefore declared "a free, sovereign, and independent State, possessed of all the rights, powers, and functions of government."

The Constitution is like that of the United States, beginning with a "Declaration of Rights," and containing articles and sections headed "Legislative Powers," "Executive Powers," "Judicial Department," and "Miscellaneous Provisions."

The Hon. John J. Roberts was elected first President of the new Republic, and inaugurated on the first Monday in January, 1848, and Liberia entered the family of nations.

This important event took place twenty-five years after the landing and settlement of the first emigrants. The people were fresh from slavery, without knowledge and without experience. Is it to be wondered at that they have made many mistakes? It is a wonder that they have not made more. The Pilgrim Fathers landed on Plymouth Rock in 1620. They had generations of civilization and experience in government behind them. They were fresh from the schools and the universities of the foremost civilized country in the world. Other emigrants of similar development followed them. The Huguenots who settled in South Carolina, and the Cavaliers who established themselves in Virginia—these men, who laid the foundation of the original Thirteen States, were educated; and they were not poor. They established schools and colleges out of their own resources; and for one hundred and sixty-three years, five generations, their communities were colonies and dependents of Great Britain. British brains and capital laid the foundation of American growth. European companies, commanding millions, interested themselves in the people and the new country, and took a hand in its practical development. It was not until at least after five generations that an independent Republic sprang up on American soil. And this Republic was not the result of peaceful concession, but it sprang from the blood of an awful contest, in which the descendants of the Pilgrims, Huguenots and Cavaliers, and enslaved Ethiopians showed themselves able to stand alone! Liberia, having never been properly developed by invested capital, set up for herself in the first generation, before her people had unlearned the lessons of slavery, or acquired an intelligent comprehension of the problems which underlie all successful national life.

The Republic is exclusively a Negro State. White persons can not now become citizens or hold property in Liberia. It is seriously argued that the country will not prosper until this obstacle is removed, and citizenship and the rights of property be open to all men. As the Constitution and the laws are now, white men will not invest their capital, as they can not protect it as citizens of the country.

There is a movement now on foot to enlarge the privileges of foreigners, so as to encourage them to make investments. It is proposed to allow them: (1) to trade and do business anywhere in the Republic. Now they are confined to the seaports, called "Ports of Entry." They are not allowed to establish factories or stores up the rivers, or in the interior: (2) to lease land for a long term of years, perhaps ninety-nine. Now the limitation is twenty years. Such an innovation would certainly encourage the investment of foreign capital, and would energize the Republic.

The condition of most of the towns and settlements shows the pressing need of enterprise and capital. Often have I stood on the top of Cape Mesurado and looked down upon Monrovia, with its wide streets crossing one another at right angles. Cattle and sheep would be grazing and children playing, and we would be delighted at the sight; but it was distance that lent enchantment to the view.

Passing through the town one sees the ruins of buildings everywhere. The costliest houses have been abandoned to the lizard and the snake; and cows graze where

EX-PRESIDENT ROBERTS' RESIDENCE.

beautiful gardens and shady walks once were. Houses propped up by poles, or falling to decay, rise up before us in vivid memory. If we turn to the streets, and to the lots containing the ruins of abandoned houses, we wonder how the people of Monrovia can live amidst such surroundings with such apparent content. In his Inaugural, delivered January 7, 1884, President Johnson said: "I think I should offend our national honor were I to omit to call your attention to what has been the state of the streets of the capital during the past year. Their bad condition has been notorious. Our national self-respect dictates that we should devise some measure by which the streets of the metropolis may be kept in a state that will comport with the dignity of the nation." Monrovia needs to be rebuilt. Its old dilapidated houses should be torn down. Such a residence as that of ex-President Roberts', which was built a generation ago, is not seen anywhere in the Republic nowadays.

Early one morning I passed up the Stockton Creek through a dense mangrove swamp. After an hour's row on the narrow stream, I found myself gazing with rapture and delight upon a broad expanse of water clear as crystal, "beautiful as a sea of glass." The banks of the river are high, and are covered with a dense but variegated and brilliant foliage. It is the St. Paul's. Up, up, I went, passing through a country that is beautiful beyond description, seeing evidences of agricultural thrift, with here and there dilapidated buildings and abandoned farms; until the name "Millsburg" is pronounced, and I ascended the banks from my canoe, and began a four-mile tramp to Arthington. Millsburg was once one of the most flourishing towns in Liberia; but now it is a deserted village. Some one calls it "a graveyard."

I passed over hills and through dales. It is a charming country. I imagine myself there now. It can not be described, at least I am not equal to the task. Coffee and sugar farms are on every side, some stretching far and wide. The majestic cotton-tree towers high, and looks smilingly down upon the graceful palm. The shrubbery, flowers, and grass are attractive to the eye, presenting every variety of color and form. The beautiful birds sing amidst the leaves, or flit across my path as if to show their gay-colored dress. Standing upon one of the highest hills, looking over the country, listening to the roar of the St. Paul's dashing over the cataracts that impede navigation, I have wondered where in all God's universe could one see a more beautiful sight. As I look away into the distance, I see houses scattered here and there. It is Arthington, bosomed in the green hills alone!

There is nothing about the place to describe. It is a settlement rather than a town. Its people are healthy, industrious, prosperous, and happy. *It is the leading settlement in Liberia.* Fifteen years ago the place was a wilderness. Mr. Robert Arthington, the wealthy manufacturer of Leeds, England, wrote to the American Colonization Society, offering to donate one thousand pounds sterling, or five thousand dollars, toward sustaining a settlement in the interior of Liberia which would be the beginning of a line of settlements to extend across the continent, connecting the East with the West Coast, Abyssinia with Liberia. The place named after the distinguished philanthropist resulted from this offer. A colony of emigrants from North and South Carolina headed by June Moore and Sol Hill, of Union County, South Carolina, plunged into what was then a primeval forest, slept on the bare ground, while their wives aided them in the work of clearing the land and building homes.

I have listened with astonishment to their thrilling story. How the men's hearts failed them when they found themselves set down in a barren wilderness! The women—and they told me themselves—felt home-longings for a moment. But a heart-wrench, and they were gone; and like heroines, they settled down to do or die! They inspired their husbands with superhuman power. They bravely shared the inconveniences, hardships, sufferings, and perils of the wilderness. But now sitting in their comfortable homes, many said to me with honest enthusiasm and pride, "I would not return to live in America if I could." They live in neat, comfortable houses. They have prosperous churches; there is an excellent school supported by Edward S. Morris, of Philadelphia; there are thousands of acres of land under cultivation; and they are pushing further into the interior. In December, 1883, the young men of the settlement held a meeting and resolved to form a colony and push further back towards the interior. Brave young men. In other parts of Liberia, they seem to be content to clerk for a pittance, to get into the Government service, or to loaf "until the old man dies." Then they move into the paternal home, and live on the accumulations of the fathers, and let things run down!

Arthington is a model place. An election was pending. A candidate, I was told, sent up to the settlement goods for distribution, hoping in that way to secure votes. The bribe was returned, and the vote of the settlement was solid against that man! If one could see the energy and industry so characteristic of the people of Arthington more general in the Republic, he would become an enthusiastic colonizationist. This thriving settlement shows that carefully picked pioneers in interior settlements can

SETTLEMENT ON THE ST. PAUL'S RIVER.

direct and control and utilize the native material, and through it develop the country. The conditions for the future prosperity of Liberia are found in Arthington. Its people seek Christian education, follow industrial pursuits, and fuse with the natives.

CHAPTER XV.

MISSION AND EDUCATIONAL WORK NEEDED.

AFRICA has the strongest claims upon the benevolence and generosity of the world. Her early civilization has been of great value to mankind. She protected the Christian religion when Herod threatened to destroy its divine Founder. By unrequited toil, suffering, bonds, and death, Africans have put the whole world under lasting obligations.

"The Dark Continent" needs the aid of Christians to reach the light of divine truth. Into their hands it places its claims growing out of its ancient service, and the injuries of modern slavery. Remembering, however, the great work recently done by Christians in abolishing the slave-trade and in emancipating the slave, Africa kneels at the feet of the true "Holy Catholic Church," and appeals for continued sympathy and help in the name of her benighted children.

The appeal is not in vain. The attention of the world is turned toward the African Continent; and the interest in its civilization and evangelization grows greater every year. The lethargy and darkness of ages are certainly disappearing in the light and activities of a Christian civilization; and in spite of the inroads which Mohammedanism is making, Africa will be conquered for Christ, God having promised to give unto His Son the heathen for His inheritance, and the uttermost parts of the earth for His possession.*

We believe that God's purposes toward Africa are great beyond conception. The Rev. Dr. Elder, of New York City, has said that the Negro in Africa would have in coming time a purer religion than materialistic America. Rev. Dr. Withrow, of Boston, has said that the sons of Ham would yet become the custodians of the sacraments and institutions of the Church. The eminent and scholarly Prof. Joseph Cook says to us in a personal letter, " The capacities of the African people, in religious directions, may very possibly some day be found to exceed those of the Anglo-Saxon race."

While we would not be led by these expressions into the indulgence of vain fancies, yet we truly believe that if materialism and agnosticism should ever be incarnate in a Herod—if they should ever seek the young child to destroy Him—the land of Ham will nourish and protect Him even as when there came wise men from the East to Jerusalem, saying, " Where is he that is born King of the Jews?" And Christianity will again find refuge in Africa, there to abide until God shall bid her come forth. The reader may not agree with Cook, Withrow, and Elder. He may not understand the fact which we now assert, that there is a wide-spread and deep feeling among Negroes that God may yet, in a mysterious way, use Africa to preserve " the faith once delivered unto the saints." It is not our purpose to exalt the possibilities of this Continent and its people. We simply plead that a race with

---

* Psalm ii. 8.

such religious potentialities and faith should be brought in contact with the Bible, so that Christ may be the chief corner-stone in the civilization of the future. Such a civilization will be superior to that which flourished in ancient times in the Nigritian and Nilotic regions, because it will be neither material nor pagan. It will be strong in its power to lift men up. It will be stronger in its power to make men humble, childlike, in honor preferring one another, Christlike. It will be aggressive, but benevolent. It will be strong as iron, yet pliable as steel; great as a giant, yet little as a child. It will know its strength, yet it will recognize its weakness. It will be the perfection of Christianity.

The African Continent is white for the harvest. Liberia is *the* gateway to this vast region, which we call Central-Tropical Africa. The Republic is known to Christian Negroes everywhere, and especially in the United States. And, although millions of Negroes do not believe in colonization, yet Liberia has the hearty interest of all; and Negro ecclesiastical operations will enter Africa through the Republic. Liberia will be our base of operations—the interior our objective point.

Much has already been done by Negro agencies, operating in and through Liberia. Thousands of the natives have been given the English language; thousands have acquired a taste for our civilization; many have embraced it and have become Christians; and a few are now preaching the Gospel of Christ to interior tribes. Liberia has not existed in vain. Christian philanthropy has done much in sustaining missions and pushing educational enterprises.

Most of the evangelical denominations are doing missionary work in Liberia. The Presbyterians were the pioneers. Such men as Archibald Alexander, the scholarly and pious first dean of Princeton Seminary, inspired his Church to enter this field. His great name and burning zeal for the evangelization of Africa have been commemorated in the Alexander High-School of Liberia, which has done much good in the country. There is a Presbytery of West Africa.

The Baptists, with great zeal and wisdom, inaugurated their missionary work very early. They lead all the other denominations in Liberia in vigor and self-reliance. Receiving less foreign aid than any other denomination, yet they have the most flourishing churches.

The Methodist denominations are largely represented; and the Missionary Societies of the United States have spent thousands of dollars in educational and evangelical work; but it has not proven to be an encouraging field.

The Episcopalians have prosecuted work in Liberia with amazing persistency and great results. Their Educational Institute at Cape Palmas and their school at Cape Mount, have reached and benefited hundreds of natives. Recently a scholarly and pious colored clergyman, Rev. Samuel D. Ferguson, was elected Bishop of Cape Palmas and Parts Adjacent, thus practically establishing Liberia as a diocese. This will give new life and energy to the cause of Episcopal missions.

For twenty years and more a board of philanthropists in Boston, and one in New York, have prosecuted missionary educational work in connection with Liberia College; but the condition of the country and the people have not been favorable to great success. It is proposed to inaugurate an Industrial Department in connection with the College. Such a movement would be a blessing to the people of Liberia.

No body of Christians have been more fortunate than the Lutherans. They have sustained for years a labor manual school and mission near Arthington, and have reached hundreds of natives, converting and enlightening them, and teaching them the art of systematic labor with the hands. The Rev. D. A. Day has been the most successful, practical worker that Liberia has received from any source. He has been in charge of this work, called the Muhlenberg Mission, for twelve years, and he seeks to make his beneficiaries self-reliant and his work self-supporting. He enlightens and Christianizes the natives, then teaches them how to work, and settles them on a piece of land, and thus starts them in the way of practical living.

At Arthington there is a private missionary school, supported by Edward S. Morris, of Philadelphia, and named in honor of his mother. From what I saw when there it is doing much good, reaching both natives and Liberians.

There are several other mission schools; but the educational facilities are few and poor. Of the Americo-African children not ten per cent. are in school; and of the entire native and Liberian population not one per cent. is receiving any instruction. The Government is too poor to educate the children. Help must come from some quarter. What a needy and inviting field.

There are in Liberia more than half a million of people who believe in a "Good Spirit," but who blindly worship Him, having their altars erected unto "the unknown God." They read the open book of nature, the towering hills, and the sloping valleys, studded with majestic trees and beautified with gemlike flowers. They read "the starry garden of the firmament—those flowers of the skies budding with the hopes of immortality." They read the gentle sunshine and the furious storm, the flashing lightning and the rumbling thunder; and they see, written as with a pen of fire, "*There is a God.*" And then there is another writing, to these natives as mysterious and as inexplicable as was that upon which Belshazzar gazed—"*Christ Jesus came into the world to save sinners.*" These thousands of souls dwelling

A MISSION SCHOOL.

in Liberia are puzzled as they read. Ask them, "Understandest thou what thou readest?" and the earnest reply is: "*How can I, except some man should guide me?*" * A burning appeal comes from Africa to the whole Church, and particularly to that part of it most able to help because of the possession of consecrated wealth and a mature civilization. In one of his preludes, in Tremont Temple, Boston, Mass., Joseph Cook sought to arouse the civiliza-

---

* Acts viii. 30–31.

tion of the Western world to a sense of its responsibility in this matter. He said: "The light of the Occident can not be hidden from the Orient. A spiritual unity is coming to the whole human family; and I would have the head feel its responsibility; and the Occident is the head of the earth and the hands of it. Nearest to God, let us transmit the spark of scientific supernaturalism into the civilization of the whole planet, and so make its reeling form stand upon its feet and worship God."

The African cry for help has reached the hearts of thousands of Negroes in America, and especially in the United States, and some have even gone, and they are still going back to the "Fatherland," to labor as teachers and as missionaries. And they should be greatly encouraged and heartily sustained by those who think that Negroes, who are fully equipped for the work, are to be the redeemers of Central-Tropical Africa. God seems to have written this truth in history and experience, that the men and the forces which act directly on the elevation of a people are of the people themselves—bone of their bone, flesh of their flesh, blood of their blood. Byron's line,

"Who would be free, themselves must strike the blow,"

applies to intellectual, moral, and spiritual as well as to physical emancipation. The redemption of Africa must come largely through the Negro himself. We say largely, because we do not believe that the work has been exclusively committed to the Ethiopian. My impression is that much of the success of Mohammedanism lies in the fact that its missionaries are Negroes. The Africans hear a simple Gospel from the lips of men of their own race. It is our opinion that white men will never evangelize the Ethiopian. The natives do not separate the white race into Christians and sinners. They regard them all as representatives of the Christian religion. The white missionary preaches Christ and holy living; the white trader cheats, swears, ill-treats six days in the week, and on the seventh occupies the chief seat in the synagogue. At luncheon in England in 1883, an eminent Englishman, who had held a very high office in India, and had served Her Majesty in South Africa, said: "We English people are counteracting, are paralyzing our missionary efforts by sending rum and opium to pagan nations"; and then, with an earnestness that I shall never forget, he deprecated the fact, and expressed the hope that God would in some way put an end to such an anomalous and sinful condition of things.

It is not to be wondered at that the Catholic cathedrals and monasteries have fallen into decay in the Congo Valley. The Church was stabbed and killed by her Spanish slave-holding children. No wonder that the tipsy African replied to the rebuke of the white missionary with the question, "Be he no your brudder who bring us rum?" The evangelization of Ethiopia will be wrought out by converted Ethiopians. I do not exclude white men, nor European and American influences altogether; but they will act indirectly in the great work, perhaps we might say directly, so far as it will inspire, aid, and guide Ethiopic energy. Bishop Crowther and his Negro followers have done a wonderful and an effective work on the Niger. Out of America consecrated and properly trained men and women will go from year to year to the "Fatherland" to work for the elevation of a race and the redemption of a Continent.

Upon all who engage in this great cause, directly or indirectly, Livingstone's prayer will be answered. He died in Africa on bended knees. He lies asleep in Westminster Abbey. When in England I stood with reverence at his grave, and read with emotion this his last prayer, cut on his tomb: "May heaven's rich blessing rest on every one—American, English, Turk—who helps to heal this open sore of the world." That is, "who helps to suppress the slave-trade and put down domestic slavery; uproot idolatry and establish pure homes, commerce, and education, and found permanent Christian institutions in Africa." The work of healing goes rapidly on. Soon Ethiopia shall rise from her reclining position, and take up her bed and walk. Among the wise men from the East, she presented to the Infant Redeemer "gifts; gold, and frankincense, and myrrh."* Through Simon of Cyrene, she bore the cross for Christ in His hour of deep humiliation and human weakness.† Through the eunuch converted under Philip's ministry, she proclaimed her belief that "Jesus Christ is the Son of God";‡ and soon, under the inspiration and in the strength of this faith, not one, but millions of "Ethiopia's blameless race" will go on their way rejoicing.

CHAPTER XVI.

AMERICAN INTEREST IN THE AFRICAN REPUBLIC.

THE Americo-African Republic has a claim upon the Government of the United States, growing out of the fact that in its incipiency it was a *quasi* colony of this country. The purchase of land and the planting of the

---

* Matt. ii. 11. I have seen paintings in Holland and Belgium of the visit of the Magi; and in every one an Ethiopian is prominent.

† Matt. xxvii. 32.   ‡ Acts viii. 37.

first settlement on the West Coast of Africa was in accordance with an Act of Congress, passed March 3, 1819. It seems to me that this nation with its seven millions of Africo-Americans will not leave Liberia alone in her efforts to get firmly established as a Christian Republic on the West Coast of Africa.

The colored people of the United States have good and sufficient cause for their interest in what millions of them call their "Fatherland." The elevation of the African Continent and the advancement of the colored American will have a reflex influence one upon the other. I believe that there will always exist on this continent a homogeneous nation composed of a heterogeneous people. The Africo-American, the Anglo-American, the Celt, the Teuton, and the Semitic races will ever dwell here in national harmony, but with racial differences. I grant that American environments will operate to transform the races. True, the American Negro will be a different man from the African Negro—different in complexion, different in physiognomy. There are great differences among Negroes even in Africa. The Anglo-American is not in all respects like the Anglo-Saxon; nor do people in the South of Europe exactly resemble those in the North. But modification is not the *differentia* of race. The changes will not be those that grow out of a sweeping amalgamation of races of men. If we examine carefully the population of the United States and Canada, we find that the different species and races of men are moving largely in parallel lines now as they did two hundred years ago. We find that Anglo-American, Africo-American, Scotch, Irish, German, and French make up the population in increasingly relative proportions. In Great Britain, the Irish Celt is as distinct from the Saxon, as he was seven hundred years ago. The Saxons and the Slavs remain distinct in Eastern Prussia. The Teutonic and the Slavic elements in the Austro-Hungarian monarchy, are no nearer mixing than they were generations ago. If there is no amalgamation between species of a similar ethnical fibre, my belief is that there will be none among races differing as do the Ethiopian, the Mongolian, and the Caucasian.

In theorizing as to the absorption of the American Negroes, we should remember the wonderful absorbing vitality of the African race. The favorite cry of colored orators is this, "We are not dying out." They ought also to say, "We are not bleaching out." More white blood has gotten into our veins in the past than will enter it in the future. The dominant feeling among Negroes is against amalgamation. Hence the systematic slighting of a man or a woman, who in the exercise of an inalienable right, steps over the race line to marry. The weight of feeling among leading white men is against a physical amalgamation of the races. They stand for the preservation of an individual's right of choice in marriage. They stand for an intellectual, religious, and political assimilation — all races dwelling together in an equal brotherhood under one American flag; but they go no further; and this is significant.*

But waiving all opinions as to the ultimate results of this American problem, the fact will not be disputed, that for generations yet unborn the Africo-American will be a distinct species of this rapidly increasing population. Our future strength and standing among the other American races will be materially aided by the redemption of our Fatherland. We can not ignore the claims of Africa upon

---

* See Cable's "Silent South" in the *Century* for September, 1885.

us, and lay broad and deep the foundations of future respect and power.

What Negro can read the history of South Africa without feelings of indignation against the white men who have enacted such cruelties there? Who of us can hear of the ability and bravery of Zulu and Ashantee statesmen and warriors without a thrill? Who can visit Sierra Leone, or Liberia, and not see with the eye of faith that the coming years will put National wisdom and wealth behind the Christian Negro, even as they are behind the Caucasian and the Mongolian? When a great Christian Negro Nationality shall speak to the world, as I believe under God it shall, the Negro everywhere will no longer be treated as a man to be despised, or to receive pity, sympathy, or toleration; but he will be regarded as an object of interest and respect, because he will no longer represent slavery and degradation. He will be identified with a people strong in its civilization, and powerful in its nationality. Is this time never to come? Is the answer, No; it will never come? Then let the Christian Negro speedily bleach out, for slavery has robbed us of our race instincts, our self-reliance, our pride!

I do not advise emigration to Liberia; and yet, I would rejoice to see a voluntary movement to the Republic of independent, self-reliant, and self-supporting people with capital behind them. We expect to see hundreds go out to teach, to preach, to pursue the professions, and to engage in commercial pursuits. These will have exceptional opportunities that their education and money will command. We have truthfully said that Liberia needs men and capital. We have drawn a true picture of the obstacles to be encountered in settling in Liberia from climate and other difficulties to be met in any new country to which capital is not attracted. I have written my *Impressions* truthfully, without fear or favor, because I have felt it to be my duty to give a correct account to those who want to hear my opinions in these matters; and because I would forewarn those who may go to the West Coast so that on their arrival they may not be disappointed, but may settle down to the trying work before them with an earnestness and a steadfastness that conquer success.

Men who expatriate themselves to gain "a better country" deserve great credit for enterprise and courage; hence I believe it to be the duty of every Negro to give at least sympathy to those who leave the land of their nativity to spend and be spent in efforts to build up a Christian Negro Nationality in the "Fatherland." They are heroes in a great battle. They are pioneers in a great work. "The blood of the martyrs was the seed of the Church." The blood and sweat and tears of our African emigrationists may be the seed of a glorious heritage for generations yet unborn.

I am not a colonizationist, because it is not my conviction that the Negro has no chance to attain here in the United States the full measure of American manhood and citizenship. But be this as it may; the colored people can not afford either to ignore Africa or to be indifferent to her claims for sympathy and service. We are already profiting by the progress of African civilization; and thousands of us are rejoicing that Africa has come so wonderfully to the front within the last twenty-five years; that its map is no longer of black ink; but that almost over its entire surface are seen great cities, commercial centres, partially civilized tribes, and powerful governments; that trade is bringing the Negro of Central-Tropical Africa face to face with the best civilized methods and the most modern improvements, and that he is Africanizing and using them with wonderful ease and rapidity. No one can tell the changes that will take place in the next quarter of a century. Steam has brought Africa within a few days of Europe. Within ten years, Liberia, now more than a month off from New York City, will be brought within ten days of the great American metropolis! Steamships will run between New York and Monrovia. Capital will go to cultivate the soil, bring to light the mineral resources of the country, and develop its general industries; and thousands of civilized American Negroes of enterprise will follow it as emigration from Europe follows capital to the United States.

Within the next quarter of a century Negroes should have their own vessels on the ocean running from New Orleans, Savannah, Charleston, Baltimore, and New York to Monrovia, Sierra Leone, Grand Bassa, Sino, Cape Palmas, the Gold Coast, and the Congo. Negro merchants and shippers should do a large business in the leading Atlantic seaports. Soon Negro capital should send at least a brig to carry our civilization in the form of workers for Africa, and to carry tobacco, cloth, hardware, and provisions to Liberia, and to bring thence the riches of that favored land. God speed the day. It will give a new impetus to industry in Liberia and to enterprise here. Do you think me a dreamer? Remember that "the evolutions of fact are sometimes stranger than the romances of fiction." Such a day will come. Aye, it must come. Negroes, even now, while they cling to the Bible and put the fear of God as first and best, yet are discontinuing the song,

> "Man wants but little here below;
> Nor wants that little long."

By the acquisition of consecrated wisdom and wealth, and by its proper use, they desire to bring to earth the kingdom of heaven; and this spirit gives us faith, push, and enterprise.

While regretting her weakness, let us not forget that the Republic of Liberia is a fact. Among the nations of the earth she is recognized and received. Her name is found everywhere in connection with the *status* or characteristics of other States. I take up a commercial work and look at the list of nations that have vessels on the ocean; Liberia is there. I examine the list showing the monetary units and standard coins of the different countries; Liberia is there. Her past career has not been altogether fruitless. Although a weak ally, yet she aided England in suppressing the slave-trade; and she would, if she had sufficient strength or influence, totally destroy domestic slavery among the natives. She has given to hundreds of natives a knowledge of the English language; and although it is spoken poorly, yet even far back into her interior it is possible to find some one among the aborigines who can speak our English tongue. She has also imparted to the natives what she could of her habits of industry; and she has given of her Christianity to many of them, some of whom are teaching and preaching unto their pagan brethren.

While I am no enthusiast over the Americo-African Republic, yet I could not truthfully say that it has existed to no purpose. I think that the planting of Liberia has helped to some extent the work of African civilization.

If in the future the United States Government should

take a livelier and deeper interest in Liberia; if foreign capital should enter the country: if a national system of industrial education should be vigorously supported; if, as a result of these, the aborigines should be civilized and educated; and if an intelligent and hardy population from America should fuse with them and plant and sustain settlements extending into the interior—then out of this Americo-African Republic, which President Monroe planted, civilizing and Christianizing influences shall sweep into the Soudan, throughout the Niger and into the Congo; and under a mighty African ruler, there will arise a stable and powerful Government of Africans, for Africans, and by Africans, which shall be an inestimable blessing to all mankind.

THE END.

www.ingramcontent.com/pod-product-compliance
Lightning Source LLC
Chambersburg PA
CBHW020147170426
43199CB00010B/932